Er

EVERY
A FAMILY GUIDE TO RESISTING PORNOGRAPHY
BY DAN S. SPENCER III

"Dan Spencer's new book, *Every Parent's Battle: A Family Guide to Resisting Pornography*, is a practical and important resource for parents seeking to protect both themselves and their children from a society saturated with distorted and harmful messages about human sexuality. Dan's book provides Catholic and other parents with tools and strategies that are aimed at prevention, rather than recovery, in the spiritual battle for the virtue of chastity. It is with hope and a deep belief in parents' love for their marriage and children that I heartily recommend this book for your family's happiness and the joyful embracing of life and dignity offered to us by Jesus Christ."

— Archbishop Joseph F. Naumann,
Archdiocese of Kansas City in Kansas

"The Roman Empire was a pornographic society — with all the misery that implies — but our own society is far worse. History shows that this problem can be overcome in only one way: the way of the Christian family. Dan Spencer shows us, in practical terms, what that means for us as parents. Reading this book is not just a good idea. It's a duty."

— Mike Aquilina, EWTN host and author of
*Seven Revolutions: How Christianity Changed the World
and Can Change It Again*

"Slavery comes in many shapes and sizes, one of the ugliest of which is addiction to pornography. This particular form of slavery is so powerful and pervasive in our deplorable epoch that it takes a particularly brave man to tackle it. Dan Spencer is such a man. In this powerful book, *Every Parent's Battle*, he pulls no punches in challenging parents to fight this war against the dragon of pornography, fighting fearlessly to prevent their children and millions more from falling under its demonic spell."

— Joseph Pearce, Director for The Center for Faith and
Culture at Aquinas College in Nashville,
editor of *The Austin Review*, and best-selling author

"As a five-time Major League Baseball All Star, I knew what it took to be one of the best in the game: hard work, mental toughness, and preparing to beat my opponent. As a father, husband, and follower of Jesus Christ, I wanted to be the best but I often failed seven out of ten times — like I did in the batter's box — in relation to sexual purity. I worked hard, had mental toughness, but I never 'prepared to beat my opponent.' Dan Spencer's new book, *Every Parent's Battle: A Family Guide to Resisting Pornography*, gives parents like you and me the tools to address and 'beat our opponent' in the alluring, evil world of pornography and sexual impurity, not only for us but for our wives and children whom we are called to lead to heaven. May this priceless piece of art be the tool you use to BE THE BEST!"

— Mike Sweeney, Kansas City Royals, Hall of Fame

"*Every Parent's Battle* may be one of the most important parenting books of our times. As uncomfortable as it makes us, we cannot deny the truth that the prevalence of pornography in our culture threatens to destroy our families and infect our children's souls. In this book, however, Dan Spencer offers more than just the hard-hitting truth. Spencer offers hope, encouragement, and the practical tools every parent needs to wage war against the destructive force of pornography. Do not despair! We may be called to battle, but there is hope for triumph over the evils of pornography, and this book is a powerful weapon every parent needs."

— Danielle Bean, publisher of *Catholic Digest*

"In *Every Parent's Battle*, Dan Spencer takes up one of the most disturbing — and important — topics of our time. He brilliantly diagnoses the pandemic nature of the problem and provides action-able antidotes to keep our families safe. This book is an indispens-able tool that should be read by all parents."

— Kevin Lowry, husband, father of eight children,
and author of *How God Hauled Me Kicking and Screaming
into the Catholic Church*

"In this book, Dan Spencer clearly explains the dangers that pornography poses to today's Catholic youth. He also provides practical steps to help parents protect their kids at all stages of development. This book should be in every Catholic parent's library."

— Peter C. Kleponis, Ph.D., SATP-C

"Families are in serious trouble, and Dan Spencer has written a wonderful book to counter the negative influences of our over-sexualized culture. His new book, *Every Parent's Battle: A Family Guide to Resisting Pornography*, is a must-read and a wakeup call for all parents that will inform and equip us to fight back for the sake of our children. I strongly encourage you to buy copies for yourself and your friends!"

— Randy Hain, author of *Journey to Heaven: A Road Map for Catholic Men* and *Joyful Witness: How to Be an Extraordinary Catholic*

"*Every Parent's Battle: A Family Guide to Resisting Pornography* is a volume full of powerful tools to help parents raise sexually healthy kids in a pornified culture. By drawing broadly on his personal experience and the depth of Church teachings, Spencer does an excellent job of providing a holistic battle plan for combating the far-reaching effects of porn in American culture by starting in the most winnable place: the home. The content, while sobering, is essential for parents, grandparents, soon-to-be parents, or anyone who desires to help the next generation of the Church to walk in faith, joy, and purity. I recommend this book to anyone who has the courage to join the fight for sexual wholeness in our world."

— Todd Bowman, Ph.D., Associate Professor of Counseling, Indiana Wesleyan University

"Practical, insightful, and timely, *Every Parent's Battle* offers parents a blueprint for leading the fight in protecting our families from the societal plague of pornography. It's a battle we as parents dare not lose."

— Matt Fradd, Integrity Restored

"There have been many books and articles written on the subject of how parents should and must deal with the sexual education and protection of their children. Dan Spencer in this easy-to-read, brief book pulls together from multiple resources the problems and dangers to parents as well as children from our sex-saturated world. He deals with the concrete issues and how to preemptively protect our children with a point-by-point plan for assuring that Catholic values on the sacredness of human sexuality are taught and understood."

— Deacon Vince Eberling, Archdiocese of Miami, Florida

"Every Parent's Battle is an excellent resource for any parent looking to protect their family from the pornography virus that has infected our country on an epidemic scale. It is jammed full of practical tools and resources that parents can deploy on day one, which are moored in the bedrock of Catholic moral teaching. For any mom or dad who has decided to proclaim, 'As for me and my house ...' *Every Parent's Battle* is an absolute must-have."

— Tony Collins, founder of King David's Rock apostolate and originator of the Temple Guard porn accountability app

"Every Parent's Battle is a book every Catholic parent needs to read and take to heart! Dan Spencer boldly addresses a topic that is silently destroying the hearts and minds of many Catholic children. As a counselor and speaker on this topic, I have heard from Church leaders that the majority of teen boys from good Catholic families are regularly using hardcore pornography. Pornography is on the rise for girls in our Church as well. Dan's book is a much-needed resource for parents, grandparents, Church leaders, and teachers!"

— Sam Meier, M.A., L.P.C., Archdiocese of Kansas City in Kansas, counselor and My House diocesan anti-pornography initiative ministries consultant

EVERY PARENT'S BATTLE

A FAMILY GUIDE TO **RESISTING** PORNOGRAPHY

DAN S. SPENCER III

Our Sunday Visitor

www.osv.com
Our Sunday Visitor Publishing Division
Our Sunday Visitor, Inc.
Huntington, Indiana 46750

About the Author

Dan S. Spencer III is a writer and speaker on topics as varied as faith, evangelism, sexual integrity, faith in the workplace, fatherhood, and the arts. He is the immediate past Executive Director of the National Fellowship of Catholic Men, a board member of the annual Men of Valor anti-pornography conference, a cofounder of the Catholic Business Network, and the founder of the Project Patriarch, an apostolate for men over fifty.

He has spoken to thousands of men and women at conferences, parish events, and parent groups across the United States and internationally. He has appeared on numerous EWTN television programs as well as EWTN and Vatican radio on the topic of fighting pornography.

Dan and his wife, Linda, have been married for forty-two years. They are the parents of four married adult children and grandparents of eleven grandchildren under the age of six. They live in a suburb of Kansas City, Kansas.

Dedicated to my cherished wife, Linda, and her tenacious commitment to the Catholic faith, marriage, and family. Parenting together has been a high adventure, unimaginable without you at my side.

Contents

Foreword

Pornography addiction is an epidemic in America. Millions are affected by it, and Catholics are not immune. It's damaging individual lives, marriages, families, and careers. It affects men and women, small children and the elderly. When I began specializing in Internet Pornography Addiction Recovery ten years ago, few people wanted to talk about it. It was still a taboo subject. Fortunately, many people are now ready and willing to confront this issue.

While anyone can fall prey to this addiction, youth are most at risk. The largest single population of Internet pornography users is teens between the ages of twelve and seventeen. The average age when children are first exposed to hardcore Internet pornography is eight. This has devastating long-term effects on individuals and society as a whole. Pornography is warping young people's view of sexuality and relationships. It's teaching boys that it's okay to use women for their selfish sexual pleasure. It's teaching girls that in order to get and keep a man, a woman must look and act like a porn star. In addition, pornography leads young people to believe that the physically dangerous and emotionally degrading sex it portrays is normal and healthy. Those who are exposed to pornography early in life are more likely to become sexually active earlier than those who aren't exposed to it.

Young people are most susceptible to pornography use and addiction because of their widespread use of technology. Whenever a new gadget or app comes out, young people tend to be the first to utilize it. Pornographers are well aware of this. Whatever the new technology is, you can be sure that pornographers will find a way to use it to get their products into the hands of young people. Their goal is to get as many young people addicted as possible and as early as possible. This ensures the pornographers lifetime customers and a steady stream of income.

Because of the dangers of pornography, there is a great need for a resource to help Catholic parents protect their kids. Dan Spencer has answered that need with this book. Most parents would readily admit they want to protect their kids from pornography, but when it comes to understanding just how accessible it is, many parents are naïve. They are probably aware of pornography on the Internet, but they are not aware of all the ways technology can be used to access pornography. They are also at a loss about how to protect their kids online. After all, it's no secret that most kids and teens are more technologically savvy than their parents.

Every Parent's Battle presents practical ways to protect kids, including concrete strategies to monitor use of the Internet and technology, both inside and outside the home. Even more than Internet filters and other defensive strategies, parents need the tools to educate their children about sexuality and intimacy, and to make their homes safe places where these topics can be discussed in open, healthy ways. This book offers invaluable guidance for parents to educate kids in age-appropriate ways about healthy sexuality, emotional boundaries, and the dangers of pornography. Parents are encouraged to model healthy marital intimacy for their kids, and not to be afraid to answer questions about sex or pornography when they arise. Kids need to know they can discuss any topic with their parents without shame or embarrassment.

Not only does this book offer much needed guidance for protecting kids and teenagers from the dangers of pornography, it also provides advice for protecting adults. This includes setting standards for the use of technology, Internet protection, proper sexual education, and creating a vision for a healthy family life.

Every Parent's Battle should be in the libraries of every parish, Catholic school, and Catholic family. No matter the age of your children, this book offers practical and effective strategies to help ensure that your families don't fall prey to pornographers and pornography addiction. Immersed in Catholic theology and teaching on human sexuality, *Every Parent's Battle* is a great tool for parents who want their children to know and live out the beauty of human sexuality as God intended it.

— Peter C. Kleponis, Ph.D., SATP-C,
founder of Integrity Starts Here

Preface

Pornography is not an easy topic to discuss. That is why so many parents and even clergy avoid discussing the topic at all. It just seems too ugly, too dark and shameful. But this reluctance has taken a terrible toll on our society, and especially our families. While that reluctance has most certainly been the case for far too long, we are now, in my opinion, at a tipping point. Parents like you must deal with this issue head-on. That is especially true given that the scourge of pornography has become a nearly universal threat to our marriages and children. It is part of an enormous multi-pronged attack on the family, and there is no opting out if you love your family — and I know you do.

Like many maladies we face as families, it remains on the back burner until it strikes at our personal lives. Unfortunately, as millions of families *are* now being impacted, most find themselves scrambling to fix the problem rather than having put strategies in place to help prevent the problem in the first place.

This passivity must change. There is great hope for protecting our families from much of the problem, but it comes with some serious challenges for parents. For all our societal claims that sexually oriented topics and discussion are no longer any big deal, the research tells us something different.

The middle school health class "talk" simply won't cut it anymore — if it ever did.

By the time I came to really understand the issue, my four kids were grown and out of the house. I can and have, however, shared what I have learned since they are all now parents themselves. I encourage them all to embrace the tools and strategies now at their disposal.

My grandmother used to say, "You can't put an old head on young shoulders." Perhaps not entirely, but in this book I am trying to share some of what I have experienced, learned, witnessed, and heard from professionals, porn addicts, and other parents that might be of benefit to you and your family. You can win this battle with God's grace and some healthy, loving parenting. God bless you and your family.

— Dan S. Spencer III

Part One

EXPLORING THE BACKGROUND

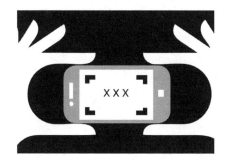

CHAPTER 1

WHAT HAVE WE BECOME?

A few years ago, an expensive ad campaign was about to be launched in Australia. Slated to appear in all the glossiest and best magazines, it was guaranteed to generate a great deal of money. At the last instant, however, the campaign was not only pulled, it was actually banned. Why? Because the ads depicted a tangle of barely clad bodies in a way that seemed to condone rape or at least to glorify an aggressive type of group sexual activity. The ads were by Calvin Klein, who has never shied away from trafficking in highly eroticized images.

Klein, by the way, is far from alone in believing that the best way to market clothing is through near nudity and the graphic portrayal of sexually charged situations. Among others, European designers Dolce and Gabbana often employ a similar approach. They once got into hot water in Spain with an ad campaign that was almost identical in style and content to Klein's, except that their ads contained not just images of young women being sexually exploited but those of young men, as well. The Spanish ads, like the Australian ones, were eventually pulled, a fact that seemed to mystify the designers. At a loss, they concluded that Spain must be "a bit backwards."

Perhaps they were a bit backwards, at least by American standards, for we do not pull such ads. We allow them to run in all their tastelessness. In fact, images that once would have been considered sordid and even pornographic now appear in the magazines we leaf through in dentists' waiting rooms and supermarket checkout lines. Nobody tries to hide them. Although shocking to earlier generations, such images have lost their power to evoke shame or cause embarrassment. Once-taboo images now barely ruffle a feather.

We know that magazine ads are not the only indication that things have changed. In the dim days of antiquity (when I was a boy) there existed a venerable store named Abercrombie & Fitch that sold sporting goods. Actually, it didn't just sell such merchandise; it was the gold standard when it came to such things. For generations those who wanted the best in hunting, camping, boating, or other kinds of outdoor-sport equipment flocked to Abercrombie & Fitch. Over its long history Abercrombie outfitted Theodore Roosevelt, who was very fond of safaris and similar wilderness expeditions. Other presidential patrons were Dwight Eisenhower and John F. Kennedy. John Steinbeck also shopped there, as did Ernest Hemingway and (oddly enough) Greta Garbo.

Abercrombie & Fitch closed its doors in the late 1970s, the victim of shifting tastes and a changing economy. However, the store was reborn in 1988 — sort of, for this supposed rebirth presented us with an Abercrombie in a very different incarnation, one that was completely focused on the youth market. Utterly gone was camping equipment. In its place were revealing clothes. Salesmen and saleswomen also seemed to be gone, replaced by young men and women who were obviously hired for their visual appeal. Often called "models," the new staff was as scantily clad as the law allowed, and the men were generally shirtless (and probably often cold). The store's marketing approach had been radically overhauled during its decade-long hiatus. The following quotation from the Wikipedia article on Abercrombie

& Fitch pretty much encapsulates the new approach: "The company has been accused of promoting the sexualization of pre-teen girls, for example by marketing thongs to 10-year-olds and padded bikini tops to 7-year-olds."

In case you didn't know, Abercrombie is wildly popular among children and teenagers.

From 1997 to 2003, and occasionally thereafter, the store published the *A&F Quarterly*, a cross between a magazine and a catalogue. Thick and glossy, it was overflowing with nude pictures of young men and women, most of them highly erotic. It was said that it "redefined the all-American look for teenagers," whatever that may mean under the circumstances. It was also called soft porn, and if you have trouble believing that, the following fact might convince you: to acquire a copy, one had to produce proof of age. Apparently, the store was very aware that putting such a periodical into the hands of children or young teenagers was likely to produce legal troubles — even though it was a magazine that had a back-to-school issue every year.

Then there's television, especially cable TV. We all know that the programs we watch devote more and more time to sexual topics every year, portraying casual sexual activity as not just harmless but the norm, the sort of thing that every healthy person ought to indulge in or at least aspire to. Such activity, television teaches us, never has any ramifications that last beyond an hour — or only half an hour, if we're considering a situation comedy.

Disturbing as they are, all these things are but the tip of an iceberg. The so-called soft porn of Calvin Klein and Abercrombie & Fitch, as well as that of cable TV, is surely immoral. But retail outlets and media are certainly not the total story. Over these last decades televised sporting events have produced scantily clad cheerleaders, half-time Super Bowl entertainment has featured "accidental" nudity, reality TV has given us dancing academies for children that teach pole dancing, and on and on. All of this is, however, mild when compared to what lurks below: a world that deals in dehumanization, a world that is not "soft" in any respect. I'm speaking, of course, of the destructive world of hardcore pornography. Now, this is something that has always existed in one form or another. How could it not in a world beset by original sin and an ever-increasing sense that truth is subjective? But until the recent past it was hidden away and difficult to encounter. One had to go to the places where it made its home: the seedy parts of town, the neighborhoods in which no one really lived and no one you knew ever visited.

Those days are gone. Our sex-obsessed culture has declined to limit pornography in any meaningful way. With the advent of the Internet a couple of decades ago, pornography was liberated from its dirty book stores and seedy peep show venues. These days, nobody has to leave home to find such material, for it comes to the computers that sit on our desks, the iPads in our bags, the smartphones we're never without. In other words, it's available 24/7 at the click of a button — and it's not just the hands of adults that click those buttons. The hands of our children — especially our sons — are adept at it. With the click of a mouse, they put their innocence at risk, not realizing how easily it can be stolen or how difficult it is to take back.

We must do whatever we can to limit our children's exposure to sexually offensive material.... Despite what you may have heard — there are definitely things we can do!

As parents, we are the bulwark against anything that might harm our children. Therefore, we must do whatever we can to limit their exposure to sexually offensive material. Let me assure you — despite what you may have heard — there are definitely things we can do! Later in this book, I will offer various strategies that have proven to be effective shields against pornography and its damage. But right now I think we have to clarify exactly what we're up against. We must understand the enemy if we are to confront him.

First, we must realize that our culture has undergone a profound and disturbing paradigm shift. I am borrowing this concept from Stephen Covey, Ph.D., who explained it in his groundbreaking book *The 7 Habits of Highly Effective People*. We will discuss paradigm shifts more fully later, but right now I'm simply going to illustrate the concept with two events from my own life. The first occurred in 1971, when I was eighteen years old. It was in the midst of the biggest and most extensive "sexual revolution" in our nation's history. I had, by grace, escaped up to that time the vast majority of its influence. The second happened about twenty-five years later. By comparing these two experiences, I am confident you will see that our culture has undergone a paradigm shift of seismic proportions in a very short time.

So here's the first story: I had never encountered hardcore pornography at all until one evening toward the end of my senior year in high school. I had been accepted at a state university and was determined to join a particular fraternity there. To that end I had been invited to a fraternity "rush" event, which, I found out, was to be preceded by a movie. Joining a fraternity had become an important goal of mine, and I was determined to do whatever it took to achieve that goal — or at least I thought I was. The early part of the evening went well, and I assumed I was off to a rousing start.

Soon, however, I found myself in a car full of prospective pledges and fraternity brothers on our way to see the promised movie — a porn movie as it turned out. I was nervous and a little worried, but nobody else seemed to have a problem with what we were going to do. In fact, our fraternity brother hosts seemed to consider it a good and normal thing, a ritual of sorts that would help to open the mysterious world of manhood to us pledges. In other words, they thought they were doing us a big favor.

I was working at attempting to get into the swing of things, which meant suppressing my misgivings. The unspoken threat of being dropped from the fraternity's candidate list was a formidable one, so as we drove I tried to convince myself that I was on board with this adventure. Real men enjoyed porn, I kept telling myself. But did they have to? I wasn't really sure. One thing I was sure of, however, was that I was getting a little queasy — a feeling which I knew had nothing whatsoever to do with the quality of the food we had eaten. The queasiness increased when I stood beneath the theater's garish lights, and it became an internal maelstrom when I sat down in the small, seedy, rather stale-smelling theater. I looked around. There were about ten or twelve patrons beyond our little group. None of them looked happy, which meant that at least in one respect I fit in well.

Don't worry. I'm not going to tell you about the movie I saw — or, rather, partially saw, since after the first few minutes I started staring down at my knees. I grant you that my knees are not all that interesting, but at least they're not pathetic or sad, and they're certainly not degrading, and those are the qualities that struck me about the film that day. Those qualities are what I still remember more than forty years after leaving that sleazy little theater. I also remember the looks that we prospective pledges gave each other. It was hard to hold anyone's gaze for more than a second or two without looking down at the ground. Perhaps we had seemed an appreciative and slightly rowdy bunch in the theater, but as we returned to the world of reality, at least some of us grasped that we had experienced something not quite right, had participated in something shameful, or at least demeaning. There had to be a better rite of passage to manhood than this — there simply had to be.

I now know that the film I (partially) saw was cutting-edge for its day but mild compared to current pornographic fare. In fact, I suspect it would be considered quaint and inadequate to the needs of today's college-bound young men. That was 1971, after all, and we were nearly a quarter of a century away from the development of the Internet and virtually all things digital. At that time, if you asked most people what pornography was, they might talk about *Playboy* and the other more tragic versions of men's magazines that were wrapped in brown paper when mailed or when hidden behind the counters of mini-marts.

Okay, that's story number one. Now on to story number two. To get there, we have to fast forward to the late 1990s. I was married, with four wonderful kids, and I was also president of a dot-com company that developed digital marketing strategies and tools. Our clients included such big names as the NFL, NHL, NCAA, and the Rolling Stones. I admired our founder, who was a strong Christian guy. I tell you all this to show that I was a long way from that confused kid who was so eager to fit in and so uncertain as to how adults should act. This was, in fact, a "Christian business" with specified Christian ethics and patterns of behavior that were embedded in its very corporate fabric. I was certainly used to the business world by this time, and I considered myself sufficiently ready for anything. As it turned out, I was wrong, for nothing I had yet encountered prepared me for the call I received one day from a potential client.

The woman on the other end of the line sounded quiet, almost shy, as she asked if we developed websites. "Yes," I responded, "we've done many." And did we also do e-commerce sites (a new development in those years)? "Yes, we've done those as well," I told her, and then I asked if she was representing a local or out-of-town firm. After a slight pause, she said she was representing herself and asked if I might have time to meet with her in the next few days. I agreed, and we scheduled an appointment. After I hung up, I really thought no more about it. As it turned out, I should have.

The day of the appointment arrived, and the receptionist called to let me know my potential client was on time. I walked to the front office to greet the visitor, a very attractive young woman, who was sitting in our reception area with her husband. The two were playing with their small son, who was laughing happily. This was going to be an unusual appointment.

As we returned to my office, she told me that she had done extensive research on websites and had decided she wanted to have an e-commerce website built. That was fine by me, so I asked the logical first question: What was the nature of her product or service? Looking me directly in the eye, she simply said "me." "You?" I asked, bewildered. She nodded as if no further explanation were needed, so I asked her to continue, and this is what I learned: She and her husband had decided to set up a personal website where she would charge people to watch her take her clothes off. The two of them agreed that a personal site would be the safest way to make significant money on the Internet at the lowest cost. To prove this assertion, she handed me a folder thick with samples of various personal sites of young women, college students, even adults who were already selling their "wares" online.

This caught me completely off guard. I was speechless, and for an instant I thought I might be the victim of some kind of bizarre joke. Certain that the woman's husband could not possibly be on board with such a plan, I turned to him with a questioning look. He simply nodded his approval, and then he actually smiled. I was mystified. We were talking about exposing his wife to the prurient stares of who knows how many men on a daily basis, and he was acting as if we were discussing a normal business plan. Men were supposed to protect their wives, not help turn them into sex objects for other men to drool over — at least that's how I was raised. Yet as far as I could tell, this "business enterprise" raised no moral questions whatsoever for either the young husband or his wife. It did for me, however, and the fact that a young child was in the room as we discussed this concept was upsetting to say the least. Wanting to protect the little boy, I asked if I might speak to the young woman alone. To my relief, both she and her husband agreed, and the child was taken by his father out of the office.

Once the two were gone, I asked the woman why she was interested in doing this. She simply repeated that it was the safest and most lucrative way to make significant money. She added that she was able to pay us a significant fee for developing the website. As she spoke, she looked me straight in the eye, and if there were any signs of embarrassment or shame on her part, I failed to detect them. As far as I could see, she simply considered herself a budding entrepreneur doing what budding entrepreneurs are supposed to do. Again, I was struck by the fact that she seemed to perceive no ethical dimension in this.

Over the next half hour, I did everything I could to convince her to change her mind, but she stood firm, and to say she was impatient with my objections is a major understatement. She told me in very clear terms that she was going to have her site made one way or another, and that she would not hesitate to take her business elsewhere if I was not interested. Aware that I was making no headway, I told her we would not develop such a website. That was the end of the conversation. Out she marched.

I felt not just helpless, but sick — far sicker than I had on that long-ago journey to a porn theater. I was very aware that I had encountered something new to me. Of course, I had dealt with pornography in general before that day, but I had never faced or even imagined the reality of the porn industry's reach. Meeting that young woman, however, confronted me with something I had been unaware of for too long — something that had entered my life in the form of an attractive young mother with a small child. The idea that such a person was willing to engage in and profit from the digital destruction of her own dignity was deeply depressing. The fact that neither she nor her husband even seemed able to notice that potential destruction was incomprehensible. It was, however, also undeniable. I would never think of pornography in the same way again. If ever I had believed it was simply immoral yet harmless, that illusion was completely shattered.

I wondered: Had porn really gone that mainstream? Did our society no longer consider it transgressive or destructive at all? Had we somehow gone from condemning it, to hiding it, to losing the ability even to discern an ethical dimension in it? Apparently so, for in the two plus decades that had elapsed between the time I was taken to see a "dirty movie" and the time I was asked to construct a pornographic website, porn had burst out of the shadows. It was no longer the furtive entertainment of lonely men and rowdy college boys held too tightly in the grip of their own testosterone. It had become so acceptable that it was now the province of PTA moms looking to earn a little extra cash for their families.

That meeting occurred twenty years ago. Today, things have gotten a lot worse.

CHAPTER 2

HOW DID WE
GET HERE?

How did we get into this situation — the porn-saturated world we see around us — and what we can do to extricate ourselves from it? Well, one thing we can't do is to throw the surrounding culture into reverse as if it were a car that we'd accidently driven onto a dangerous road. Like it or not, this is a road we're going to be hurtling down for a while, for as I tried to show in the preceding chapter, pornography in its softer and supposedly "more tolerable" forms has permeated our culture to the point that it has simply become another aspect of it.

This is the paradigm shift I've already mentioned in relation to the work of Stephen Covey. What Dr. Covey meant by a paradigm is the particular set of "lenses" through which we see life and experience the world. A paradigm is shared by the members of a group or culture and involves a common set of assumptions and understandings (often unexamined). It's a method of processing information, perceptions, experiences, and beliefs, a way of interpreting things and assigning them meaning. Dr. Covey calls paradigms "mental maps" that we use to navigate life.

We live in a time in which the way we understand sexuality, gender, privacy, and male-female relationships (perhaps, even, all human relationships) is in flux. In other words, we are in the midst of a paradigm shift. The way information is processed, the way we gain knowledge, and the way we communicate with others are also changing, and this means we have another paradigm shift on our hands. One way of thinking, perceiving, and understanding is being replaced by another. But this is still only a process. It has not affected everyone in the same way or to the same extent. We're on a cusp, so to speak, with some people happily embracing the new paradigm, others still firmly entrenched in the old, and many somewhere in the middle.

Parents who grew up when an earlier paradigm held sway may not grasp the shift, as I didn't when I met with the young wife and mother who wanted me to create a porn website for her. They may continue to interpret things through the paradigm they have always known. This means two things. The first is that such parents, being unable to accurately assess the dangers their children will face, may find themselves unable to protect their children at the very times they are most in need of protection. The second is that such parents will not be able to *equip their children* with the tools needed to deal with this new paradigm.

More than a few such parents seem to be of the same opinion as my long-ago fraternity brothers: that pornography is not just an inevitability but a rite of passage that many young men — primarily but not exclusively — must undergo. Many fathers take this passive approach, and in doing so they are almost always engaged in an act of rationalization. This is frequently how it goes: A man knows that despite strong parental instructions to the contrary, he regularly perused men's magazines like *Playboy* when he was an adolescent, and he knows most of his friends did the same. He figures (probably quite correctly) that his own son is every bit as likely to disregard his instructions concerning porn as he was in disregarding those of his parents concerning *Playboy*. He is aware that he survived his *Playboy* reading without any lasting wounds and concludes that his son will do the same. Seeing this as a reasonable analogy (which it definitely isn't), dad breathes a sigh of relief. No big problem! It's just a guy thing, he concludes. "Boys will be boys," and guys have certain urges that are difficult to control, and they just have to learn to deal with them. Case closed. Time for another round of golf.

What is missing, of course, is the awareness that at its peak of popularity in 1975, *Playboy*, according to a 2016 article in *Time* magazine, had a circulation of 5.6 million. Today, more than 100 million people in the United States visit adult sites monthly.

Younger parents, however, usually assess the situation more accurately. Having lived most of their lives under the new digital paradigm, they are aware of the prevalence of pornography and of the extreme nature of what is available on the Internet (things Hugh Heffner would never have imagined). That's good. What's not so good is that, being inured to our hypersexualized culture, they may simply view such things as the new normal. Perhaps an unfortunate, but hardly sinister, reality. But a darker reality is in play in many homes.

Sadly, it is no longer rare for a father to be addicted to the very pornography from which he should be protecting his children — a situation that can open a virtual Pandora's Box of trouble. For instance, he won't want his wife (let alone his children) to know of the secret life he engages in, so he will refrain from installing technology filters on the family computer. He therefore makes it easier, and far more likely, that his children will come in contact with porn. What happens when the children stumble upon their father's Internet viewing history? They may conclude that pornography is a normal, acceptable, and even desirable part of life … or they may be repulsed and start to view their father in a different way — as a man they do not really know, a stranger.

In 2014, a Barna Survey reported these two telling statistics:

- 37 percent of Christian men and 7 percent of Christian women use porn several times per week or more
- 64 percent of Christian men and 15 percent of Christian women use porn once a month or more

That so many Christian men are currently using pornography themselves compromises their own spiritual leadership and renders them unwilling to talk to their sons.

So whichever paradigm parents currently inhabit — or even if they're straddling both — they often exhibit an unfortunate inability or unwillingness to deal aggressively with this problem. I'm beginning to think that, despite all the widespread and barely veiled eroticism of our culture, hardcore pornography may be for us a bit like sex in general was for the Victorians. It's all around us, and we know that. We also know that everybody else knows it; yet we act as if it didn't exist, as if it's something we shouldn't discuss in polite company and especially not in front of the kids.

Porn is a dark subject, but by ignoring it or pretending it doesn't really exist, we set up our children for confusion, pain, and hurt.

Perhaps that approach worked for the Victorians, but it won't work for us. I get that it's hard to talk about porn. It's a dark topic, and people naturally prefer the light. Even the most rational discussion of pornography is unpleasant and embarrassing for most of us. It is also a potential source of shame and self-reproach to those who already have fallen under its spell. Yes, porn is a dark subject, but by ignoring it or pretending it doesn't really exist, we set up our children for confusion, pain, and hurt. In other words, we fail in our God-given vocation as parents.

Until relatively recently even the Church shied away from this distasteful topic. Although she has always made it clear that pornography is sinful and harmful, like the rest of us, she has largely soft-pedaled the issue. But the Church is catching up with the paradigm change. Understanding that the pornography of today is far more accessible and far more destructive than that of the past, the Church has begun to develop an offensive. Blessed Paul VI, Pope St. John Paul II, Pope Emeritus Benedict XVI, and Pope Francis have all written and spoken boldly about the dangers of pornography, shining a spotlight on the issue and vigorously denouncing the objectification of the human being that lies at the heart of porn. An increasing number of bishops and priests are doing the same, which is a very positive development.[1]

As parents, we can only find it encouraging that the Church has begun to confront our culture's corrupt understanding of sexuality, an understanding that turns persons made in the image of God into things to be used and then tossed aside without a thought or regret.

"God did not give us a spirit of cowardice but rather of power and love and self-control" (2 Timothy 1:7).

But as we hope we must also act. As Christian parents, we are called to fight against all the things that might eat away at or cripple the souls of our children. We are to be bold, as the Scriptures say, "For God did not give us a spirit of cowardice but rather of power and love and self-control" (2 Timothy 1:7). He strengthens us through the sacraments, and we must fight with all the strength and all the resources that He provides. But to fight effectively we must know what we are fighting against. According to Dr. Mary Anne Layden, the Director of Education of the Center for Cognitive Therapy at the University of Pennsylvania, we are approaching 100 percent exposure to pornography for males between ten and twenty-nine years of age.

I would suggest pausing for a few seconds to allow that statistic to sink in. Nearly *all* of our young men from *before* puberty and into married life have viewed porn. Keep in mind that Dr. Layden is not referring to the *Playboy* of twenty years ago with its airbrushed photos and impossibly perfect bodies, as parents who grew up under the sway of an earlier paradigm might imagine. She is speaking of the graphic video presentation of nearly every sexual act of which the human body is physically capable, and she is speaking of a type of pornography that systematically degrades women.

We must not flinch from the fact that, despite how disagreeable such pornography sounds, our sons in particular are biologically "wired" for such temptation. Sexual desire, especially male sexual desire, is intense, rarely far from the surface, and very easily stimulated — and that goes at least double for very young men and adolescent boys. By the time a boy enters adolescence, he is being bombarded with the hormones that his body has started naturally producing in abundance. He is confused and buffeted by them, and no matter how much he might want to resist, he finds that he is irresistibly drawn to anything that seems even remotely sexual.

Males, by virtue of this hardwiring for visual stimulation, are by far the greatest consumers of pornography, though women and girls are gaining, and that's a disturbing fact. Since males are more easily aroused by the visual than are females, and since much, but not all, pornography deals primarily in images, our sons are more easily ensnared than our daughters. Ensnared sons are among the greatest problems a parent may face, for today's pornography is nothing short of a no-holds-barred assault on a young man's imagination, on his understanding of sexuality, on his ideas concerning how women should be treated. Our culture serves up a plethora of opportunities for a young man to encounter pornographic content regardless of his desire to avoid it. Perhaps most important, it has the potential to become an addiction with all the attendant devastation it brings, including violence directed at women. In April 2016, *Time* magazine reported: "In a study of behaviors in popular porn, nearly 50% of 304 random scenes contained physical aggression towards women, who nearly always responded neutrally or with pleasure."

Yes, I know what you're thinking. You're skeptical of my assertion about addiction: you're telling yourself that pornography cannot result in addiction because addictions develop when we take some chemical substance into the body, something like heroin, nicotine, alcohol, or caffeine. But I didn't dream this up, it's something that psychologists, psychiatrists, and neuroscientists have already asserted.

Pornography as Drug

Pornography affects the brain like a drug. New research shows that certain sexual actions, such as masturbation, produce chemicals in the brain. These chemicals — primarily dopamine and oxytocin — are generally good for us when released through normal enjoyable activities in life. They produce a sense of pleasure and bonding that, during sexual activity in a loving marriage, are healthy and natural. But viewing porn releases an overabundance of these chemicals with a frequency that is neither normal nor healthy. With frequent viewing and self-induced sexual stimulation, the brain is flooded with these chemicals. This, in turn, does two additional things: 1) It creates a craving for them in larger and more frequent doses, leading to an addiction similar to that of cocaine or heroin; and 2) porn use literally shrinks the brain.

The Changing Brain

Science has demonstrated that the human brain can physically change, an ability referred to as "plasticity." Research has shown that repetitive viewing of pornography results in an actual rewiring of the brain to accommodate the new pathways of pleasure forged during the viewing of porn and the associated behavior that accompanies it. These same neuroscientists have told us that an overabundance of these stimulating neurochemicals also shrinks the part of the brain called the frontal lobe. This part of the brain is responsible for making good decisions and for problem solving. Flooding our brain with these neurochemicals, then, impairs our decision-making and problem-solving ability, diminishing our capacity to function successfully.

There is good news, however. This damage can be reversed by eliminating the pornography viewing and related behaviors. Depending on the individual and the degree of addiction involved, a good Catholic therapist or counselor who is trained in treating porn addiction can be of tremendous help to an individual who wants to move toward freedom.

Diminishing Returns

If, however, a person does not seek the treatment necessary for a porn addiction, he finds himself in a deepening spiral of shame, disgust, and secrecy. At the same time, he typically requires increasingly higher quantities of his "pleasure drugs" to achieve the same result. This is most often achieved by viewing and responding to ever more deviant, perverse, and violent pornography for stimulation. Eventually this becomes "normalized" in the mind of the addict resulting in the pursuit of the worst sexually deviant behaviors.

The obvious conclusion is that although the use of porn may begin as a "simple" spiritual lapse or sin, it usually does not stay there; it easily and frequently becomes a life-consuming compulsion — even an addiction. Unlike other addictions such as illicit drugs, liquor, or pills, all of whose affects can be instantly witnessed by others, pornography often runs silent in a person's life for a long time without any detection.

Although men and boys are the major consumers of pornography and the ones most likely to become addicted to it, women and girls are far from immune to its effect. In fact, they are the ones most victimized. The damage done to women who perform in porn videos is obvious (according to statistics reported by former porn "star" Shelley Luben, female porn stars have a life expectancy of 36.2 years, while the published research of Daniel R. Jennings puts the number at just 37.43 years). And the problems women face in trying to build or maintain loving relationships with men who are porn addicted or at least strongly porn influenced is increasingly clear. As Dr. Jill Manning testified before the U.S. Senate in 2004, over 50 percent of divorces today cite online addiction as one of the primary causes for the divorce.

But that's not all. A new problem is emerging: the number of women who view pornography is growing. Sometimes this is because women, in a desperate and misguided effort to attract their porn-addicted husbands or partners to a more intimate life, agree to join them in their favorite indoor sport — watching porn. Other women, sadly, are asked, pressured, or even forced to watch porn by husbands or boyfriends. Still other women simply start watching it and enjoy it. All this predictably results in a disturbing and growing new phenomenon: women who are addicted to pornography.

No matter what our sinful world may suggest to us, ultimate power is on the side of goodness and decency — ultimate reality is love and *not* degradation.

Despite all these rather depressing facts, here's the most important thing to remember: pornography is not invincible. No matter what our sinful world may suggest to us, ultimate power is on the side of goodness and decency — ultimate reality is love and *not* degradation; at its innermost depth, ultimate reality (and that means God) contradicts and rejects all that porn represents. That's why I wrote this book as a call to battle, and not a lament. Our sad world can be redeemed, and pornography can be overcome, but to do so we must work, and probably work very hard.

So let's get on with it. In the next chapter, we'll gather more information so that we can better comprehend the current paradigm regarding pornography. After that we'll examine strategies to protect ourselves, our homes, and most importantly, our children. We will learn how to fight not just valiantly but effectively against a source of genuine evil.

CHAPTER 3

WHAT WE'RE UP AGAINST

We're up against a lot, no doubt about it. For those readers who like to chew on numbers, here's the financial breakdown:

Total Porn Annual Revenue from All Sources[2]

Adult Videos	$ 3.62 billion
Internet	2.84 billion
Cable TV/PPV/Phone Sex	2.19 billion
Strip Clubs	2.00 billion
Novelties	1.73 billion
Magazines	.95 billion
Total	**$ 13.33 billion**

How can this be possible? Well, think about this: In the two seconds it took you to read the previous sentence, approximately 600 people initiated a search for one of the 4.2 million pornography websites that are available. During that same time over 18,000 people began viewing one or more of the nearly half *billion* porn web pages accessible, a percentage of those people spent nearly $7,000 on porn materials — all in just two short seconds!

I assume it's beginning to make some sense now.

But how does porn make its money? That's certainly a reasonable question, and here's the answer: through seduction and ensnarement, of course. The majority of porn users begin with almost casual visits to porn websites on the Internet. Most such sites are easy to access, as they're free of charge, and this makes any number of repeated visits possible. Such sites may generate no income for their owners, but they act as what the business world would call a "loss leader." Pornographers are willing to give something for free in the hope that you will come back for more and pay for the privilege, which is precisely what happens to millions of people. They get hooked before they even realize it, and as their appetites increase for more and more provocative content, they begin to pay for access to an ever-more-stimulating offering from the pornbrokers. This transition can be quick or slow depending on the individual.

Of course, most people never make the step of paying for Internet porn, but a significant number do, and ever so slowly they become addicted. Remember that our culture reinforces this slow decline with a constantly expanding menu of porn-light offerings: yesterday's outrage is tomorrow's Super Bowl ad or halftime entertainment. In a year or so it will go mainstream, and the year after that it will provoke little more than a yawn. The number of people who become addicted or habituated to porn provides the income that sustains the industry's profits. Imagine how many people that must be to generate over $13 billion a year!

Here's another hard fact: pornography is one of the primary drivers of personal technologies including the Internet. It has been said that the Internet could not survive without pornography. Indeed, Berenice Baker of the British *New Statesman* magazine calls it "symbiotic smut" in her article of June 17, 2013. "There is a very good reason for it," the former IT executive writes, "telecom giants whose shiny new networks and successive generations of mobile services were partly funded by sex lines, often run out of unlikely locations like Peru." So the profits from Internet porn fund even the most conservative of communication firms as they reach into other areas of digital growth such as gaming.

The porn industry has actually driven many of the innovations we see today on the Internet. One of those was online payment systems. In 2001, there were an estimated 7 to 7.5 million adult pay websites.[3] By 2008, an estimated 3 million Americans purchased pornography online, paying an average of $60 per month.[4]

The first thing this information — unpleasant as it is — tells us is that at its core pornography is an industry. It is not really about sex at all, nor is it about anything else that might be human. It's about money. Despite the fact that porn's bottom line is so impressive that most legitimate industries couldn't hope to match it, porn is essentially lifeless — tricks conjured up to make you part with your money.

Happy marriages and, by extension, other happy, meaningful relationships often have a limiting effect on porn consumption.

Now let me give you another statistic, but this one will *encourage* you: happily married men are 61 percent less likely to look at porn than are single or unhappily married men. You don't have to be a statistician to realize that's an immense difference, and you don't have to have a doctorate in psychology to figure out what accounts for it. I believe that in that difference we find a powerful weapon against the seduction of pornography. Happy marriages and, by extension, other happy, meaningful relationships often have a limiting effect on porn consumption. That only makes sense: However misguided and destructive the use of porn may be, it always involves a search and often a profound yearning for connection with another — for the human contact that it is our nature to crave. Pornography perverts this longing and pretends to offer what the soul desires, yet it can deliver nothing in the long run but frustration, sorrow, and loneliness.

Real relationships, marriages, parenthood, and deep friendships satisfy at least one of the longings that drive many people to the fleeting and imaginary relationships they find in pornography. Porn thrives in a culture that has become atomized, that considers relationships (even marriages) to be ephemeral and of no great meaning. I do not think it can take root as securely in a situation where family bonds and friendships are strong and long lasting. How could it? When we are deeply connected to others — when we love them — we are less able to view people like them as objects, as means to an end, and that is what porn requires of us.

As an illustration of that I offer the following story, the tale of a young father whose addiction to porn was strong, but no match for his love for his family.

> Frank was, by all accounts, a wonderful provider, father, and husband to his wife, and a guy who loved playing golf.
>
> It was on such a day, while he was out golfing, that his young daughter decided to do something special for Frank while he was at the course. She decided to clean his car and surprise him when he returned home after his round of golf. What occurred was certainly a surprise. While cleaning his car out, his daughter came upon Frank's "secret

stash" of porn videos under the front seat of his car. His daughter was, of course, horrified. She ran into the house and showed her mother what she had found. Not long after, Frank returned home.

He was bursting with joy as he rushed home to tell his wife of his success on the course that day. A record setting performance that he was anxious to share. As he entered his home, it was clear that something was drastically wrong. His wife told him what had happened and that his daughter was in her room crying inconsolably. Rather than being one of his proudest days, it had become his most horrific day for Frank. A day when a father, husband, and friend came face to face with a pattern of secrecy and shame.[5]

Today Frank, and his family, are in a good place, which is a fact that may come as a surprise. His family's reaction was a torment for him — a real horror, in fact. For a time, it seemed to shatter his life, and it was more than enough to open his eyes. He realized his use of pornography had suddenly transformed itself from a closely guarded secret into a threat to the home life he dearly loved. He also saw how dishonest he had become and grasped that he was not the man he claimed to be to his wife and daughter. He had been keeping part of himself from them for years, a part that he knew was dark and shameful. Desperate to become the father and husband his family wanted him to be, Frank sought professional help. He eventually reconciled his issues with his wife and daughter, which is, of course, wonderful.

Perhaps what is even more amazing, however, is that he told his story, through a diocesan-sponsored video, to every Catholic adult at Mass on one particular Sunday. He had become to thousands of other men and women not just the face of the harmful effects of living a life of sexual secrecy and increasing desperation, but the face of someone who had been able to overcome a deep and seemingly intractable problem. I watched the video with my wife and adult children during Mass that Sunday. I was shocked but proud of that man's courage to show the reality of porn use — and another reality, as well, that of God's power of love to break the shackles of pornography use.

Here's some more information about the effects that familial relationships can have on sexual behavior in general. Adolescents whose parents talk with them about standards of sexual behavior are significantly more likely to be abstinent.[6] Young people whose parents talked to them about what is right and wrong in sexual behavior were *significantly* more likely to be abstinent than peers whose parents did not.[7] Surely we can conclude from this that the family wields a certain power that many of us don't even recognize in the battle to protect our children not just from pornography but from all forms of sexual irresponsibility. In fact, teenagers report that parents remain the largest single influence in their lives.

Your children are not mere leaves blown from place to place by an irresistible cultural wind. As a parent, you can anchor them in both reality and morality.

Close nurturing contact and loving communication between parent and child, especially if it is accompanied by strong leadership exercised by the parent, has a powerful effect on determining the child's actions as he matures. Your children are not mere leaves blown from place to place by an irresistible cultural wind. As a parent, you can anchor them in both reality and morality.

Here is some more positive news: Harris Interactive survey found that 76 percent of adults *disagree* that viewing hardcore pornography on the Internet was morally acceptable (less than 25 percent found it moral) and 74 percent *disagree* with the thought that viewing hardcore pornography on the Internet was harmless entertainment. So, despite our culture's saturation in both softcore and hardcore pornography — despite a paradigm shift that seems to normalize pornography — about three quarters of us *still* find something immoral in porn. Despite all our culture's efforts to inure us to the dangers presented by porn, most adults can still see it for what it is.

In these facts (and they *are* facts), we can see what must be the core of the defense against pornography. In a word, it's *family*. Think of that for a moment, and you might notice something odd: family is the very thing we are trying to protect from pornography, yet it is also our greatest protection from pornography.

Part Two

STRATEGIES FOR SUCCESS

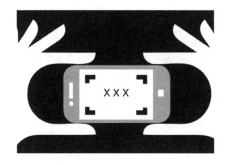

CHAPTER 4

FIRST STRATEGY

UNDERSTANDING FAMILY DYNAMICS

I'd like to begin our strategies by sharing an overall parenting guideline model from a good friend of mine, Dr. Todd Bowman, founder of the SATP Institute (www.satpinstitute.com), which deals with sexual addictions. Dr. Bowman received his Ph.D. in counseling psychology, is married, and has three children. He uses the acronym SYNAPTIC to describe issues and principles we need to consider as we parent our children, particularly our adolescent children. We will touch on many aspects of the SYNAPTIC approach in later chapters.

SYNAPTIC Sexuality Model

It is no secret that adolescence is a time of incredible growth of the sexual system. From the development of secondary sex characteristics such as facial hair in young men and the widening of the hips in young women, to the initiation of primary reproductive capabilities found in menarche and spermarche, this volatile period of growth is not without challenges. As culture evolves and the sexualization of young people occurs at younger and younger ages through exposure to media, pornography, and peers, having a working model to use in stewarding the sexuality of children and adolescents has become a parenting necessity. The SYNAPTIC Sexuality

Model incorporates the wisdom of biblical literature and the rigor of scientific literature to help parents build and maintain sexual virtues in their children.

In addition to the body experiencing tremendous change during adolescence, the human brain is also under significant transformation during these years. Raging hormones and uncontrollable emotions tend to leave our beautiful children in a state of powerful insecurity and willing to define themselves by the trends and values of their peers. With the average age of exposure to pornography continually decreasing, and video games pushing the envelope with regard to sexual content, it is only a matter of time before these children turn to sexual activity as a means of articulating their sense of identity, personal security, and autonomy. If there was ever a passage of Scripture written to address this developmental crisis, it is found in Paul's epistle to the Romans, where he writes:

> I urge you therefore, brothers, by the mercies of God, to offer your bodies as a living sacrifice, holy and pleasing to God, your spiritual worship. Do not conform yourselves to this age but be transformed by the renewal of your mind, that you may discern what is the will of God, what is good and pleasing and perfect. (Romans 12:1–2)

The journey from childhood to adulthood is one that brings tremendous joy and significant pain. Understanding how to steward — to manage — one's body, including one's sexuality, is a part of this narrative; so too is understanding the role of culture in influencing thoughts and behaviors, and finding a way to live in Christ in the midst of these pressures. With the right assistance from parents or caregivers, our children can make that journey more enjoyable and less painful by taking on the mind of Christ and living out the elements of SYNAPTIC Sexuality.

Structure

The first principle is structure. Problematic sexual behavior tends to emerge from one of two types of home environments — rigid or chaotic.

In more rigid family systems, there is little room for the growth of healthy autonomy and children can feel stifled by the invasions of parental worry or the pressure of parental expectations. A more common type of rigidity in Christian families more closely resembles scrupulosity, with spiritual perfection and sexual purity as nonspoken, but clearly communicated, requirements for acceptance.

Unfortunately, this rigidity becomes the soil out of which sexual struggles will emerge. The expectation of perfection with zero conversation about how to manage the cultural dynamics surrounding sex leaves today's adolescent in a difficult position. Many choose to deal with the tension they feel in the best way they know how: create two separate lives. They build a public self or façade that meets the demands of the rigid system, while simultaneously building a secret life where they struggle with issues such as pornography, masturbation, and other forms of sexual acting out. This establishment of the façade is a building block in the development of a sexual addiction.

Chaotic family systems also tend to produce adolescents who struggle with sexual behaviors. Adolescents who come from rigid systems develop a façade to maintain a sense of acceptability; adolescents who are raised in chaotic environments use sexual behavior as a mood-altering experience, an approach that is also predictive of later sexual addiction.

Chaotic environments tend to be defined by the absence of parent-child engagement, or a style of engagement that is volatile, inconsistent, and unpredictable to the child. There may be rules or expectations about sexual behavior, but they are never enforced. Sexual behaviors are found early in chaotic environments, often due to early exposure to sexual content, and are adopted as a primary mechanism for reducing stress, feeling in control, soothing pain, and numbing sadness, pain, and shame. Managing big emotions with sex, however, fuses their sense of connection to others with sexual gratification and has an inherent objectifying quality to it.

Healthy family environments tend to predict that adolescents will have fewer sexual partners, will wait until later into adulthood, ideally marriage, before beginning intercourse, and are less likely to divorce in later life. One key feature of healthy environments from a sexual perspective is that parents have resolved their own sexual stories and are able to be open, clear, and thorough with their children about the meaning of sex from a biblical perspective. The structure that we create as parents has a significant influence on how our children will negotiate their sexual development.

Yielding to Accountability

Given the assault on biblical definitions of sexuality in recent years, the pressure facing adolescents to conform to the attitudes and beliefs of culture is unprecedented. Some school districts provide curriculum and teaching about human sexuality in ways that are completely contrary to God's design for sexuality. In short, it is impossible for our kids to walk this journey of sexual purity alone. Helping them yield to accountability is an essential step in helping them be good stewards of their sexuality.

One type of accountability that is necessary in the twenty-first century is some type of Internet accountability. Adolescents and teens sometimes operate with the best of intentions, but their best intentions can still fall short of what is appropriate for their sexual development. In fact, because they are citizens of the online world, pornography is actively seeking them out, even if they never go looking for it. There are many monitoring products available, but Covenant Eyes, from a Christian company, has features that allow Internet blocking and filtration to adapt and grow with your family as children age.

Parents need to practice one-on-one accountability, too. That is, fathers must have open dialog with their sons about pornography, masturbation, sexting, abuse, and every other sexual topic. Likewise, mothers should be intentional in talking with daughters about the aforementioned behaviors as well as such topics as their menstrual cycle and date rape. Making sex a topic of healthy conversation while their children are young gives parents' significant influence in shaping the decisions that teenagers make when their parents are not present. In addition, encouraging adolescents or teenagers to discuss their sexual struggles with a trusted spiritual director or priest is an important form of spiritual accountability that can help support the messages being given in a Christian home.

Novelty

We are created to explore, and discovering new things excites us a great deal. Our capacity for creating beautiful things is one way in which we reflect the majesty of our Creator God. This powerful truth can operate in a redemptive way in our children's sexual development by giving them a sense of reverence for their emerging sexual drive; it can also be the energy that drives them into problematic exploration of sexual activity and the resulting physical, emotional, and spiritual consequences.

With regard to our drive toward novel experiences, we exist in a culture that emphasizes breadth of exposure over depth of knowing. For example, in some theological circles people have a very broad definition of who God is, but in their searching out the periphery of who He might be, they miss out on knowing Him more fully and completely. Likewise, there are others who know God very specifically and deeply, but miss out on the fullness of who He is given their overemphasis on one part of Him. This need to hold a tension between breadth of knowing and depth of experience translates well to a framework for helping adolescents understand godly sexuality.

We need to communicate to adolescents
that we are designed to place parameters
around our sexual relations in the covenant of
marriage, with our spouse intended to be
our only sexual partner.

Specifically, we need to communicate to adolescents that we are designed to place parameters around our sexual relations in the covenant of marriage, with our spouse intended to be our only sexual partner. In creating this boundary around the breadth of partners, real or virtual, the marriage is able to grow into greater depths of spiritual and emotional intimacy.

At the same time, sexual intimacy as a form of connection is not intended to be the only form of knowing and being known in the marriage relationship. This message runs counterculture to the depictions of relationship in media of all sorts. But parents should help adolescents understand that God's design for novelty means knowing Him and our spouse more intimately, not trading out sexual partners or viewing sexual imagery online.

Affect Regulation

The inability to manage emotion is a common feature in a variety of sexual struggles. This difficulty in finding healthy ways to modify one's mood leads to the use of sexual behavior as a mechanism for changing from sadness, stress, frustration, disappointment, fear, emotional hurt, physical pain, guilt, shame, or any other feeling to a state of calm. As well, many teens report using sexual experiences as a way to move from a state of boredom or lack of feeling into a state of being able to feel some emotion. While disturbing to admit, pornography, sexting, and video chatting each offers a world of fantasy where pleasure, acceptance, and desire are available at the touch of a button.

When it comes to raising sexually healthy children, helping them become aware of their emotions is an important place to start. Parents who are in touch with their emotions and express emotion in a healthy way model good emotional health and have a tremendous influence on how their teens navigate the sometimes unpredictable world of adolescent emotional turbulence.

In addition to being able to identify their emotions, teens need to have healthy outlets for them. Emotions that have been stuffed tend to leak out in unhealthy ways, namely with sexual or aggressive acts. Behaviors that help children manage big emotion are an essential part of a child's tool kit, enabling him or her to achieve healthy relational and sexual functioning in later life. Spiritual disciplines — reading the Word, time in prayer, time in worship with singing, and time in fellowship with other believers — are a great tool for managing emotion, as are exercise, playing instruments, sports, art, and other hobbies. The more options for managing emotion that can be put in place, the less probability that the adolescent will go foraging into sexual behavior in an effort to find a sense of emotional peace.

Physical Activity

Video-game culture has done as much to shape adolescent sexuality as pornography, although not in the ways one might think. One part of this equation is the changes in neurological functioning that can take place with binge playing of video games. In fact, the *Diagnostic and Statistical Manual of Mental Disorders*, Fifth Edition, published by the American Psychiatric Association, now includes Internet Gaming Disorder as a possible diagnosis. Features that can emerge with hypergaming lifestyles include difficulty concentrating, impulsivity, emotional dysregulation, and anhedonia, or loss of pleasure in typically enjoyable activities.

The brain regions responsible for these functions are still developing during adolescence, which can explain why teenagers can seem so unpredictable at times. These features are also common among folks struggling with problematic sexual behavior. So teenagers who do not possess fully developed neurobiology get a double whammy when their lifestyle includes a variable such as video gaming, which can create further difficulty.

Video gaming is also having a significant impact on sexual development because of the increase in sexual innuendo and outright sexual activity in certain games. At best, the sexual act happens off screen, but it is implied; at worst the individual playing is responsible for controlling the sexual behaviors of the character on the screen, complete with full nudity in some instances. This, taken with the fact that porn culture and video game culture are extremely entangled, means gamers will likely be introduced to sexual materials at some point in their play.

Physical exertion and exercise, however, increase blood-flow to the regions of the brain responsible for decision-making. Getting the body moving, rather than sitting sedentary for hours at a time playing video games, helps the body decrease stress levels so that children and teens are better able to manage emotion, generate personal insights, find creative solutions to problems, and achieve a stronger overall sense of personal well-being. While exercise it not a cure all, it can be an excellent tool for establishing physical, emotional, and spiritual health.

Touch

Healthy physical affection is missing in many American families. We know that physical touch is essential to the physical survival of infants — in its absence an infant can experience a phenomenon known as failure to thrive. Unfortunately, as children age into the awkwardness of their adolescent years, parents can feel increased discomfort in knowing how to connect with them physically.

Are your children seeing you model healthy nonsexual physical touch?...
Are your children experiencing healthy non-sexual physical touch from you?

Much like physical activity, touch is a powerful form of emotional regulation. Holding hands has been shown to lower blood pressure, synchronize breathing, and decrease resting heart rate. It is a powerful bond of connection. Similarly, hugging for thirty seconds initiates a neurological chain of neurotransmitters and neuropeptides that are responsible for helping us feel calm, connected, and trusting. Given the importance of touch, we can ask ourselves two questions: 1) Are our children seeing us model healthy nonsexual physical touch? and 2) Are our children experiencing healthy nonsexual physical touch from us?

When there is no modeling of non-sexual physical affection in their parents' relationships, it is easy for adolescents to sexualize their own relationships with the opposite sex. If they are not getting the physical touch they are created for from a parent or caregiver, they will take the comfort and connection they crave from whatever source will give it to them, even if that means participating in behaviors that they know are wrong. Touch is a necessary ingredient in raising sexually healthy kids.

Touch, however, does not stop at the physical level. Spiritual and emotional touch are vital in helping adolescents feel heard and understood, which is an important element of bonding. Spiritual touch includes letting our children know we are praying for them, or even better, praying with them. It also means ensuring their "mind diet" includes some type of Christian formation. A healthy spiritual diet includes worship experiences with same-aged peers, instruction from the Scriptures in the form of a homily or sermon, participation in the Eucharist for those who confess Christ, regular engagement in the sacrament of confession, and some form of service to others.

Emotional touch involves intentionally creating a sense of trust and connection in the parent-child relationship through skills such as monitoring tone of voice, engaging in eye-to-eye contact when talking, softening facial features to communicate empathy and understanding, and repeating back what has been said. Not only are these skills valuable for your parenting tool kit, but most marriages can benefit from incorporating these behaviors on a more regular basis.

When questions about sex and sexual behavior come your way as a parent — and as you talk about healthy sexuality, there is an increased likelihood that they will — how you respond becomes a significant predictor of how (and if) future conversations happen. Keeping the lines of communication open means maintaining influence as our kids grow, change, and navigate the sexualized culture around them.

Intentionality

"Intentionality" — a sense of purpose — is a commonly overlooked aspect of raising sexually healthy children. All too often, parents are quick to provide a response of "because I said so" to the difficult questions or situations that their children face. A similar response is to defer to the Bible and say, "The Bible says it is wrong," or some variation thereof. While a step in the direction of the Bible is a step in the right direction, adolescents, who are immersed in the process of determining the values they will live by into adulthood, need to hear a more complete explanation for why we as Christians believe what we believe and how that impacts our sexual ethics, which in turn determine sexual behaviors.

When we model intentionality in our lives and in our parenting, it is a small step to help our children capture this same intentionality in their sexual development.

Perhaps the greatest malady of the twenty-first century is boredom. While there is unprecedented access to literature, art, educational materials, music and film-making software, you name it, all available at the click of a button, there is also an unprecedented sense of meaninglessness and boredom among youth today. Boredom paired with a lack of direction or purpose is a perfect storm of variables from which sexual foraging can emerge.

Whether traversing in less than appropriate parts of the Internet or pushing sexual boundaries in a relationship, boredom tends to make adolescents operate like mindless robots, driven by their hormones and underdeveloped sense of behavioral management. While our kids need to learn how to manage the inevitability of boredom, it is a sense of purpose — intentionality — that will help them steer clear of foraging for sexual stimulation in these moments.

Connection

There are four primary dimensions to connection: with God, with self, with others, and with creation. These are echoes in the greatest commandment, which Jesus states in Matthew 22:37–39: "You shall love the Lord, your God, with all your heart, with all your soul, and with all your mind. This is the greatest and the first commandment. The second is like it: You shall love your neighbor as yourself." At its very core, sexual intimacy is about connecting with one another in a way that deepens our understanding of God's love for us. However, the messages from culture about sexuality have robbed adolescents of this understanding.

Helping adolescents live in sexual purity begins with helping them establish a vibrant relationship with Christ.

Helping adolescents live in sexual purity begins with helping them establish a vibrant relationship with Christ. When they have a personal relationship that provides a sense of meaning, direction, and identity, and they see it modeled in us as their parents, they have a strong foundation for conducting themselves with sexual integrity as they engage the world around them.

This personal relationship with Christ provides adolescents the benefit of seeing themselves as God sees them. Rather than focusing on the shortcomings or deficiencies that can be highlighted by trying to fit into mainstream culture, which are sometimes evidenced in comments about the shape of one's body or their style of dress, adolescents who know and like themselves tend to be more secure in their personhood and less inclined to move toward sexual activity as a means of garnering attention, acceptance, and love. As Christ states in the previous passage, loving others as yourself suggests there is a healthy connection with self as a launching point for empathy and compassion. As we help our adolescents love themselves in godly ways, we provide them with a secure base from which they can reach out and love others healthily.

Lastly, love for others becomes a multifaceted construct when it is an extension of an adolescent's ability to love and feel secure within themselves. Specifically, they are able to grow in their capacity to define relationships more with *phileo*, or brotherly love, and less with *eros*, or erotic love. This notion of companionate love is important, helping us view others not as objects to be consumed, as typically seen in pornography and emulated in many relationships in American culture, but rather as "others" who need to be loved as Christ loves.

The ability to form and maintain healthy connections is internalized by adolescents as they develop: whatever they have experienced with us is what they will re-create in their own relational worlds, good, bad, or ugly. As we model grace, we disciple them into a better understanding of God's love, which equips them to become more fully who they have been created to be, and to love others more completely as a result.

CHAPTER 5

SECOND STRATEGY

BEGIN WITH THE END IN MIND

Can anyone achieve a significant goal without first being clear on what that goal is or why it's important? It's theoretically possible, of course, but I doubt it's very common. We are likely to achieve difficult objectives only when we see them clearly, focus on them carefully, and yearn for them so intensely that we're willing to make real sacrifices to attain them. I would go so far as to say that realizing an important goal takes not just good planning but genuine passion.

It has become nearly axiomatic that if you fail to plan, you plan to fail. This is true for individuals and groups, and it is true in spiritual and temporal matters. A person significantly improves the odds of experiencing a successful outcome when a plan involves long-term strategies and shorter-term action steps. Jesus himself recommends (see Luke 14:28–30) that you count the cost before you begin to build.

Since we, as parents, find ourselves in a spiritual war against a pornified, eroticized culture and the toxic reality of pornography, we would be wise to engage in some strategic thinking, planning, and actions.

To be successful in our efforts, we, like a pole vaulter, need to back up and get a running start. That begins with having a clear vision of what we want to actualize in our family life and with articulating a specific mission to accomplish that vision.

Family Vision

A family vision statement provides a mental picture of an optimal desired future reality. It is the North Star that guides all of our efforts daily as a parent in relationship to our children. It also helps us fashion action strategies and steps that are in alignment with our vision.

"Avoiding pornography" is not a vision statement.

In fashioning a vision statement, a family should consider the fact that God has ordained the family as the primary place in which children are educated about the moral truths necessary for human happiness and eternal life and where the faith is modeled.[8] With this understanding, parents can begin to consider what steps they should take to accomplish this larger goal, especially, for our purposes here, in terms of its implications for sexual integrity.

I would suggest parents create a family vision statement such as:

> *That every member of our family spend eternity in heaven together.*

Assuming such a family vision is in place, we then move to our specific *mission* and its various components, all of which must be in alignment with that vision.

Family Mission

A family mission statement differs from a family vision statement in that it seeks to answer three key questions about the family: 1) What the family does; 2) for whom it does it; and 3) how it does it. I would suggest parents consider and create a family mission statement such as:

To create and mutually support a strong Catholic family culture, where each family member successfully lives an integrated Catholic life led by faithful parental modeling, mentoring, and protection

Finally, with these two statements in hand, parents can begin to identify, implement, and build a faithful Christian worldview for the family as a whole and for each individual family member. The following strategies and action steps will help each family embrace its vision and mission in the area of sexuality.

Achieving the Goal

Obviously our most immediate goal includes finding ways to keep pornography far from our homes, and especially our children. On its own, however, that will never be enough. Our primary goal must be more than merely constructing some kind of moat to protect us from the dangers and debasements of the world.

We do *need* that moat, and it must be as wide and deep as we can possibly make it (that means you must be intentional about it). But we must accept the reality that in today's world it will never be unbreachable. Short of keeping our children virtual prisoners in our homes with no access to any modern means of communication, we cannot guarantee complete protection from the endless reach of today's porn.

Our goal ... as it relates to sexuality must be to develop within our children *internal* perspectives and defenses that enable them to see the lure of pornography for what it is, and to reject it.

Our goal, therefore, as it relates to sexuality must be to develop within our children *internal* perspectives and defenses that enable them to see the lure of pornography for what it is, and to reject it. We must provide them with the tools to understand that no matter how enticing porn may appear on the surface, it is little more than a lie and an attempt to make of them less than they were created to be — an effort to erase the image of God in which they were made.

How are we to accomplish such a colossal task? By creating a family of pure hearts, minds, and bodies; a family whose members love God and one another authentically, deeply, and consistently. A more direct way of saying the same thing might go like this: Our families should live the lives for which God actually made them. In his apostolic exhortation entitled *Familiaris Consortio*, Pope John Paul II said much the same but in still fewer words: "Family, become what you are."

To accomplish this, the Church knows that our life's journey must be one toward an ever-greater life of Christ-centered integrity — including sexual integrity. If we want to deal seriously with pornography, we must understand this concept, and we must apply it carefully and consistently to our own lives and the lives of those we love. Consider the following true (actual names changed) story.

> Cindy, 11 years old, came into the kitchen where her mother and dad were drinking a cup of coffee. She looked uncomfortable for a moment until her mother asked if something was wrong. "Yes," the young girl answered. "I shouldn't have watched the video," she said. "What video?" her mother asked, getting nervous. "Susan showed us a video of another dance academy where the 10- or 11-year-old girls were all dressed up sexy

and dancing 'weird' while a boy was inside a cage trying to grab them." The young girl then showed the video to her parents, and they were shocked at what they saw. A "respected" dance academy had put on the show, filmed it, and posted it on the Internet to promote the academy.

While the girl's parents were both shocked, they were pleased that their 11-year-old daughter had found the writhing and sexual innuendo presented as inappropriate for her to see. Pleased yet angry — they had prepared their daughter for such an attack on her innocence, but still were deeply angered by what they had seen.

Sexual integrity, when properly taught and modeled by parents, resides in the deepest part of our being, informing our every action, giving us the ability to be the people that God created us to be. The ability to be, remain, and grow in such integrity comes from the grace we receive in the sacraments and from the Holy Spirit working within both parents and their children. It speaks to our inner life and character and is expressed outwardly in many ways, not the least of which is holy sexual expression in marriage rather than in self-centered indulgence in whatever may stimulate us at a given moment.

The family, as we have said, must then adopt a family commitment and *climate* where every person in the family is safe and respected and seeks a life of spiritual integrity. The *Catechism of the Catholic Church* speaks of the need to purify the "social climate" from pornography on a societal level, but I would extend that same challenge to the home. Every home must be committed to a climate of respect and holiness where "purity of heart brings freedom from widespread eroticism and avoids entertainment inclined to voyeurism and illusion" (CCC 2525).

Freedom Fighters

The *Catechism* is telling us that "purity of heart" actually helps to produce freedom. Pornography (as we have said), on the other hand, chips away at our freedom, destroying it bit by bit until almost nothing is left but a pile of broken possibilities.

Here's a fact: We find real freedom when we act in accord with our God-given nature. Yes, believe it or not, it's really that simple. Freedom grows when we act in harmony with God's will.

Chris Hedges, a journalist who has written extensively about pornography, puts it this way: "Pornography does not promote sex, if one defines sex as a shared act between two partners.... It promotes the solitary auto-arousal that precludes intimacy and love."

Real persons cannot exist in porn. In fact, reality itself cannot exist in porn, especially the reality of a full, integrated, vibrant human life.

Now tell me the truth. Does that sound like freedom to you? I would imagine that for most people it doesn't. Porn can tolerate no affection, for affection humanizes, turning a source of sexual stimulation back into a person — and real persons cannot exist in porn. In fact, reality itself cannot exist in porn, especially the reality of a full, integrated, vibrant, human life.

I hope you're beginning to see that pornography involves not only a loss of integrity and freedom and a flight into unreality, but it is the antithesis of love. No matter how much excitement it promises, in the final analysis it will leave us disintegrated, bereft, empty, and alone, held spellbound by a flickering digital screen.

I encourage all parents to think of yourselves as nothing less than the "architects" of your family's future. You are the ones who must create an environment that makes sexual integrity, and indeed all personal integrity, possible. You and your spouse must work to build a family with a particular set of values and virtues that constantly point beyond yourselves to that for which you were made. This does not depend only on the construction and maintenance of a moat, but also on a worldview that informs your thinking and your practices on a daily basis.

Ultimately, you must understand the context in which you operate and the purpose for which you donate your lives to your children. Ignore the culture's life goals for your family!

If employed consistently, this approach — a vision and a mission — will produce results. It's no quick fix, and it's not perfect, but it's a real hope.

PARENTS' PERSONAL REFLECTIONS

- Do the ideas about purity, chastity, or sexual integrity feel old fashioned or out of date to you? Do they make you uncomfortable? Do they sound silly or meaningless? Do they sound unattainable?

- Did your family of origin talk directly, euphemistically, crudely, sensitively, or at all about sexuality? How does that affect your attitude toward pornography, if at all?

GROUP DISCUSSION

- Do you think most couples find it difficult to discuss sexual topics, especially pornography? Why?

- What fears or reservations, if any, do parents have about discussing pornography with their children?

- For many, words like purity and chastity are tough to describe. Read and discuss CCC 2517–2527.

ACTION STEPS

- Create your own Family Vision and Mission Statements.

- Discuss the ideas of purity and chastity with your spouse. When you are both satisfied that you're on the same page, decide on a definition of purity that you would both feel comfortable with as your family standard.

- Identify the particular sensitivity that each of your children might have to sexual terms and issues and discussion. Decide which parent would be best suited for each of these discussions.

RESOURCES

Good News about Sex & Marriage, Christopher West, St. Anthony Messenger Press.

Men, Women and the Mystery of Love, Edward Sri, St. Anthony Messenger Press.

Create in Me a Clean Heart, United States Conference of Catholic Bishops (USCCB), www.usccb.org.

CHAPTER 6

THIRD STRATEGY

EMBRACE PARENTAL LEADERSHIP

The issue of drug use and abuse has gained a great deal of attention in society, and has led to considerable success in educating our children about and protecting them from the dangers of drug use. But what of pornography? Does it receive the same scrutiny and protection? The answer is emphatically no. There is no war on porn as there is a war on drugs. There are few institutions that actively seek to limit the exposure of children and young people to pornographic material.

In other words, you're going to have to accept a difficult fact: there's very little leadership out there in the culture that will guide you in protecting your children. That means that *you're* the one who has to do the leading.

The Catholic Church has made it clear exactly who is responsible for leading when it comes to the topic of sexuality. It isn't the state. It isn't even primarily the parish. The Pontifical Council for the Family, in its document *The Truth and Meaning of Human Sexuality*, says that "the role of parents in education [about the purpose, benefits, and growth in chastity] is of such importance that it is almost impossible to find an adequate substitute." Other social challenges may have found their champions in public outcry, industry

sanctions, and even governmental regulations. Unfortunately, pornography is not following that same path.

Okay, I understand that's not what you wanted to hear.
Maybe you should sit down and take three deep breaths before we continue, but continue we must, and the first thing
we have to do is ask what kind of leader you need to be. I
always answer that question the same way when I speak to
parents — and especially mothers. Do you remember Sarah
Palin's colorful line when describing the difference between
a pit bull and a hockey mom? The distinction she drew was
simple and to the point: "Lipstick," she said. That's the kind
of leader you have to be: ferocious and implacable. It's your
children you're protecting, after all.

Okay, okay, if the image of pit bull wearing lipstick
is too much for you, try thinking of Joan of Arc. She'll do
just fine — better, in fact, for she pursued victory single-
mindedly, and she trusted completely in God to enable
her to do what no one thought was possible.

Many skirmishes in your war against porn can be
won more easily than you imagine — *if* you display real
leadership by laying the groundwork before the enemy
ever shows his ugly face.

By that I mean that if parents make a genuine and
consistent effort to discuss sexual matters in a forthright
but age-appropriate way with their children, those children will grow up feeling comfortable with such discussions. They will be far more likely to tell you about any
contact with porn they may have had (not to mention any
other kind of sexual contact), and they will be far more
open to following your advice concerning it, for they will
have come to see you as a source of sexual information
that can be trusted. We'll discuss such strategies in our
next section, but we must clearly understand that passivity
will not get it done.

There is an abundance of evidence showing
that children of parents who are aware,
proactive, and diligent do not suffer from
the same level of exposure to pornography
that others do.

There is an abundance of evidence showing that children of parents who are aware, proactive, and diligent do not suffer from the same level of exposure to pornography that others do. The willingness to discuss sexuality in a realistic but reverent way is an irreplaceable part of being "aware, proactive, and diligent." So it's probably time for you to bite the bullet and begin those little talks.

Yes, I agree that it's no fun, especially if you've avoided it so long that those conversations will produce the embarrassment and discomfort characteristic of adolescence rather than the easy acceptance of children too young and innocent to be self-consciousness about their body parts and processes. But if you fail to exercise leadership in this regard, you're making the job of protecting your children from porn more difficult than it has to be.

Statistics show that only about one in four parents has had a basic discussion about porn with their kids even after those kids have entered their teens. There are no statistics that show the amount of harm that particular lack of communication causes, but I suspect it is significant. I often wonder how much of that harm could have been avoided by a few heart-to-heart conversations between parents and children.

Breaking the Cycle of Silence

I know that large numbers of parents find it hard to speak to their kids about sexuality at all, let alone pornography.

Too many avoid it, hoping against hope that the typical seventh-grade health class talk will magically do the trick (it won't, and it never has). When I speak at conferences or parishes regarding pornography, the vast majority of parents in attendance rather sheepishly admit they have never had a direct discussion about sexuality with their kids at all.

Do you find that surprising? You wouldn't if you knew another fact that I have gleaned from these same speaking engagements. The great majority of these boomer and millennial parents tell me, when I ask, that *they* never had a clear, understandable discussion about sexual issues with either one of *their* parents when they were young.

That's right: it's not just you and your generation, but the generation that preceded you and probably the one that preceded that. It's a genuine American tradition, this reluctance to speak about sexuality with our children, let alone pornography. The disturbing result of this tradition is that many adults, having never been given a complete, faith-based overview of sexuality, have been left with no real role model to imitate in discussions with their own children.

Because of that lack you may feel like you can't manage these daunting discussions, that you're flying blind and don't know what to say or how to say it. Don't panic; I'm going to give you some guidelines in the next section, where you will find specific suggestions as to when such information is appropriate at different developmental stages. First, however, here is a little advice from the Bible: "Do not be afraid. Go on speaking, and do not be silent" (Acts 18:9). Here's some advice from me: Don't just speak; speak from the depths of your Catholic faith! God has given us our sexuality because it is a good and holy thing. When we use our sexuality as God intended us to use it, we are really involved in something sacred, in God's continuous act of love and creation.

There's no reason to avoid discussing sexuality with your children as long as you emphasize the goodness and holiness inherent in it and make very clear the things that deviate from and even obliterate that holiness. Conversations that are frank but that emphasize the sacred nature of sex and the sacred obligations that go along with it are of incalculable help in a parent's battle against porn.

Here's some more good news that holds true even if you've never spoken one word about sex to your kids: You have more influence over your children than you think you do. It's strange but true. Most parents are amazed at how much influence they have with their children, even after those kids have reached middle school. Just the act of saying "I don't want you to do that" carries far more weight than many parents think. Kids actually appreciate your saying it.

Remember, early adolescence is a terribly confusing and uncertain time. Much of that time is spent striving to figure out how adults should act and why *they* should act that way — and what that means for them. Often adolescents are given very few guideposts along the way as they try to puzzle this out. As a parent, you're the one who has to hammer those guideposts into the ground to help your children navigate the labyrinthine path to responsible adulthood. The information and guidance you give will serve as both a guidepost for your child and as solid ground to stand on. Information he gets from his friends and the Internet will most assuredly not serve this purpose.

In our technology-centered culture, the Internet is the natural place for a child to turn for sexual information if he doesn't get such information from his parents. Permitting or encouraging a child to turn to the Internet for sexual information is not just dangerous, it's begging for disaster. Virtually any search regarding sexuality will produce for that child a wide-open door to the always enticing world of pornography. You can bet the house on it.

Even if through some miracle such a search did not lead to porn, it still would not lead to what you want for your son or your daughter. Sure, there's some good information about sexuality online, but there is also an enormous amount that is not so good and an avalanche that is just plain awful. Many physicians bemoan the abundance of so-called medical information on the Internet that is actually misleading, incomplete, or simply wrong. Parents should bemoan the idea that even if Internet information on sexuality is scientifically flawless (which of course it is not), it is impersonal and absolutely lacking in a moral or religious perspective or context. At worst, it has been crafted in such a way as to promote ideas about sexuality that are strongly opposed to the ones you want to inculcate.

Teaching a young person about sexuality
is an act of love, and like all acts of love it
requires both nuance and sensitivity, a subtle
awareness of what a particular child is and is
not ready for at a given moment.

Teaching a young person about sexuality is an act of love, and like all acts of love it requires both nuance and sensitivity, a subtle awareness of what a particular child is and is not ready for at a given moment. Information alone is not sufficient, for information often consists of mere facts divorced from meaning. The meaning of that information, both psychological and spiritual, in the child's life is what the parent who assumes leadership must impart. Again, this is the sort of thing that can only be done adequately in a loving and trusting parent-child relationship. There's no such thing as a one-size-fits-all cookie-cutter approach here.

Parents who discuss simple concepts such as anatomy and birth basics with kids when they are young find it much easier to discuss pornography when those kids hit their adolescent years. An example of how this can be successfully navigated is the use of great books such as *Good Pictures Bad Pictures*, by Kristen Jenson and Gail Poyner. Since we've already seen that the average age of a kid's first exposure to porn is eleven years old (I'm repeating that because I want it to sink in), the chances are good that porn questions will be floating around in your child's head *before* puberty.

If you have proven yourself open to discussing sexual matters, he will be much more likely to take those questions to you rather than to friends or to whatever anonymous Internet resources he happens to hit on. That means you have to be prepared. This is definitely not the moment for improvisation. You have a significant responsibility to have at hand some cogent, kid-centric ways to explain the issues. In other words: Do your homework well and don't wait until the last minute.

If you're still vacillating about those uncomfortable talks, here's a piece of information that may push you over the edge. A report from the National Center for Health Statistics[9] showed that most kids actually *want* to talk to their parents about sex and related topics in the safe environment of the home. If that didn't do the trick, I'll just reiterate something I've already said: Adolescents whose parents talk with them about standards of sexual behavior are *significantly* more likely to be abstinent than those who don't.[10] Young people whose parents talked to them about what is right and wrong in sexual behavior are *significantly* more likely to be abstinent than are peers whose parents did not.[11]

Our Parental Privilege

In the final analysis, it is not just our duty but our privilege as parents to teach our children about sexuality and to make sure that our teaching is given a clearly Catholic context. To do so, we must make sure that we parents have a good, faith-based understanding of sexuality to begin with. That, by the way, may be an obstacle you'll have to overcome, as many young parents today have not had effective or consistent catechesis themselves. If you're unsure of Catholic teaching regarding sexuality, that's a problem because you cannot successfully lead your family if you're not sure where you're leading them. It is your responsibility to learn what the Church actually teaches. There are many good books on the market that can help with this and many fine priests who will clear up any confusion you might have. Christopher West's *The Good News about Sex and Marriage* is a great place to start. But make no mistake: it is *your* responsibility to acquire the pertinent knowledge that can guide you as you guide your children.

Whatever the state of your current knowledge, there are certain indispensable principles that will help you lead your war on porn. They can be formulated in many ways, but here are examples of four critical faith principles and how you might state both the principle and expectation:

- **Sexual Principle:** Christ and His Church teach that heterosexual sex is the only acceptable expression of sexuality and must be reserved for sacramental marriage. Outside of sacramental marriage sexual abstinence is required of all.

- ***Expectation:*** All members of our family shall abstain from sexual practices and behaviors that violate Church teachings or lead to the violation of the dignity of any person.

- **Marriage Principle:** God has ordained that marriage is a sacrament and forms an indissoluble covenant between one man and one woman. A valid marriage exists for life and (like all sacraments) cannot be undone. This covenantal relationship is a sign of the relationship between Christ and His Church.

- *Expectation:* The Church recognizes both internal and external pressures on individuals to cohabitate before marriage, to succumb to inappropriate reasons to marry, to enter into nonheterosexual unions, to consider civil divorce during difficult periods within marriage, or to seek remarriage following a civil divorce. She therefore presents specific teachings, guidelines, resources, and pastoral support for every situation. We are called to adhere to such help if and when such challenges present themselves.

- **Sexual Integrity Principle**: God has created the human person with inestimable value, including the beauty of the body and the dignity each person deserves by virtue of being created in the image and likeness of God.

- *Expectation:* Pornography, in *any* form is unacceptable. Under no circumstances will any member of our family engage in listening to or viewing any images or other material that dishonors the dignity of the human person in any way, but especially in a sexual manner. This includes dishonoring one's own body as well. To assist in this area, various accountability plans will be put in place for the protection of the entire family.

- **Teaching Principle:** The subject of sexuality has to be put into the context of the child's own eventual vocation, whether that be to marriage, the religious life, or single life. It is to be considered as "education in love" and commitment, rather than education in the mechanics of sexual reproduction (as the secular models usually propose).

- *Expectation:* When teaching about and discussing sexuality, there is to be no use of graphic materials that offend purity. All biological explanations will be done in an age-appropriate manner and with age-appropriate explanations and resources.

Perhaps these principles and expectations seem a little on the self-evident side. If so, it suggests you have internalized the Church's teachings to a significant extent. So much the better; you're off to a good start. If, however, they don't, or if some elements of them seem problematic, unrealistic, or even impossible to achieve, then you have to look very hard at your understanding of Catholicism, which means that you also have to look at your understanding of God and your relationship to Him. These principles are nonnegotiable. They are what the Church has always taught, and they are very tightly bound up with that purity for which we must strive. There's no such thing as cutting corners on this one.

After you have thought about the above principles, discuss them in depth with your spouse. When you do, you may find some surprises. All too often, we simply assume our spouse shares our standards completely. That may be so, but don't be surprised if you discover differences. Some of these differences might be small and relatively insignificant. Others might be large and problematic and require meeting with a priest or counselor. Whatever they are, the best time to discover them is definitely not three minutes after you learn that your teenage son is accessing hardcore pornography on his computer or your teenage daughter has been busily "sexting" with her boyfriend on the iPhone you bought her for Christmas.

In other words, if you want to deal with the problem of pornography effectively, you've got to be on the same page with each other and you've got to know what that page is. Both clarity and consistency are indispensable. That is the only way your children will know what is acceptable and what is not. Remember that the world around them will be actively undermining what you're teaching. The lure of pornography is a powerful one. Don't underestimate it. As you and your spouse discuss principles such as the ones I've included above, you'll develop a language with which to speak about such things with each other and your children.

When speaking to children about sexual issues, parents often flounder for a vocabulary that is appropriate to the situation. Sometimes they never find it and leave their child mystified or just plain annoyed. Neither result is helpful. By articulating certain terms, principles, and expectations in advance, you will know what to say when the moment comes, and you will know how to say it clearly and concisely. That certainty and clarity will send a strong and unambiguous message to your kids.

That's exactly what you want.

Whether you're vague on the Church's teachings regarding sexuality or can recite them backward in Latin while you're standing on one foot, I'm going to give you an invaluable resource for dealing with pornography and all aspects of human sexuality. It's a Vatican document entitled *The Truth and Meaning of Human Sexuality*, which was published by the Pontifical Council on the Family and is available on the Vatican website (www.vatican.va). It is relatively short (forty-nine pages), very readable, and so excellent that one priest I know actually called it "the best document the Vatican ever produced in any century," which is pretty high praise. Guess what? It was written specifically with parents in mind! What a find!

This is a document that will fill in the blanks for you, giving you a great deal of thoughtful information to pass on to your children. It carefully restores what our culture has deleted from its conception of sex (things like love, respect, and spirituality), enabling you to offer your children not just a full and true understanding of sexuality but a deeply Christian one.

Once you've navigated *The Truth and Meaning of Human Sexuality*, and if you feel you're ready for the postgraduate course on the Catholic understanding of sexuality, investigate Pope St. John Paul II's writing on the *Theology of the Body* (I recommend a basic intro edition written by Christopher West).

St. John Paul II understood the deformed and deficient ideas about sexuality that have taken root in Western culture, and he was determined to combat them by presenting the Church's teachings in all their logic and beauty. Between 1979 and 1984, he delivered 129 weekly audiences and homilies, which were collected and put in book form (*The Theology of the Body*). In his teaching, he presents us with a mosaic of the majesty and mystery of the human body and how it "speaks" to specific questions about why God created men and women. His overarching goal was to transmit to us an integrated vision of the human person as more than just a biological organism, but rather an unbreakable union of body and soul.

Some books about the theology of the body are appropriate for teens and junior high age groups. I suggest that as part of your leadership strategy you buy your children such a book and read it slowly, carefully, and (especially) prayerfully *with* them. Doing so cannot help but make porn — as enticing as it is to adolescents — appear deficient and less than worthy of a human being made in the image of God.

PARENTS' PERSONAL REFLECTIONS

- Do you understand the Church's teachings on sexuality? Do they make sense to you?

- Does your newly discovered information about porn anger you sufficiently to make you act?

- Are you aware of your child's school's stance on blocking pornographic Internet access on school computers or those distributed to the students?

GROUP DISCUSSION

- Men frequently leave it up to their wives to discuss spiritual (or difficult) topics with their children. Why is that inappropriate?

- Why is it beneficial for both parents to be seen supporting the family's spiritual and sexual standards?

- Most children know how to "play" their parents against each other in certain situations. Why and how would that be a problem when discussing sexuality/ pornography with children and enforcing guidelines?

ACTION STEPS

- Discuss any differences you and your spouse may have concerning sexuality in general and pornography in particular. Discuss how you can provide a unified front to your children.

- Discuss the best ways to speak (age appropriately) to your children regarding sexuality and pornography.

- Discuss and decide which parent (or both parents) will handle sexual education and discuss corrective matters.

RESOURCES

Theology of the Body for Beginners, Revised Edition, Christopher West, Ascension Press.

Theology of the Body & Marriage, Christopher West, Ascension Press.

Parenting with Grace: The Catholic Parents' Guide to Raising Almost Perfect Kids, Dr. and Mrs. Gregory Popcak, Our Sunday Visitor Press.

Theology of the Body High School Edition, Brian Butler, Jason and Crystalina Evert, Ascension Press.

CHAPTER 7

FOURTH STRATEGY
HOMELAND SECURITY

Okay, here it is, the chapter you've been waiting for; the one that will give you an edge in solving some of your problems. We're going to switch gears and discuss practical rather than spiritual or psychological ways to make your home and your life porn proof ... or at least as close to porn proof as is humanly possible. By now we all are very aware that we're engaged in a type of war, and our homes are the primary battlefield. How does your home-protection plan stack up against this threat? What can you do to bolster your defenses, to present as impregnable a fortress as possible? Let's explore ways to set up your own Department of Homeland Security in a way that even the most tech-challenged parent can grasp.

Technology is the primary horse that pornography rides in on. Some parents are sure they are on top of it all ... but that can also be a dangerous illusion.

Before we begin, we must accept that technology changes at lightning speed these days — a reality that can keep you off balance and often struggling to catch up. It's just a fact of life. Many parents don't feel confident around newer technology, but their children seem able to master whatever comes down the pike with no problem at all. Obviously, if you're in that situation you're at a disadvantage, since technology is the primary horse that pornography rides in on. Some parents are sure they are on top of it all — and they may very well be — but that can also be a dangerous illusion. Both a lack of confidence and overconfidence about technology can be a problem. You should strive to avoid both. Cautious realism is the key.

Now, take a moment and count up all of the devices in your home with connectivity or potential connectivity to the Internet. How many do you have and how safe have you made them in terms of blocking access to Internet porn? Sometimes, despite our best efforts, we fail to "connect the dots" of accessibility since we don't really know all the potentials of our own devices. That's because we — old fogies that we are — are often unaware of the various ways technology has changed and continues to change. I have friends who are still kind of amazed that phones can take pictures!

Digital Gateways

We'll begin by talking about your television and your access to the Internet, which are the most obvious points of entry for porn. I'm willing to bet that for some readers, at least, this section will contain a surprise or two. The majority of homes today receive Internet and cable TV from the same provider. Each carrier then pumps digital signals into our houses using fiber optic or copper cable on a single line. That single line enters a box somewhere in your home called a router, which then acts as an antenna to broadcast Internet and TV signals to all of the devices in your house. You must be aware that there are no inherent filters in any of this. Whatever is available on the Internet also becomes available to the devices you have. It's like a flood of information and images that sweeps through a pipeline into your home unimpeded. Your job, clearly, is to do the impeding.

To accomplish that, you should know some basic information about things like browsers. Why? Because approximately 99 percent of all pornography in the world is accessed over the Internet, and to get on the Internet, computers rely on software called browsers. Become familiar with the browsers utilized by the devices in your home. Note that it is possible to have more than one browser on a device. The most common that come factory-installed on PC devices include: Internet Explorer, Firefox, Mozilla, Safari, and Google Chrome. I'm sure you're familiar with the names.

You should also be familiar with the fact that each company that produces browser software has its own way of handling security. Each has browser-specific methods of allowing parents to filter and block adult content. It's your job to learn as much as you can about the browsers that are installed on your devices. While we may not be able to keep pace with the often opaque language of computer engineers, we can be familiar with the basic tools they have given us to begin protecting our kids. It isn't necessary to understand the microdetails, but rather the macrosystems and the concept behind those systems.

Now let's move from a discussion of browsers to one of television. If we were speaking face to face, I'd imagine you'd look confidently at me and say something like this: "Yep, we're good there. We have the TV locked down. The kids can't even see adult themed titles, let alone access the content."

Perhaps that's so, but your television might be trickier and more dangerous than you suppose. Why? Because any TV sold since 2012 is actually just a computer with a monitor. They *all* come equipped with wireless Internet capability. Most have You Tube, Vimeo, Daily Motion, and other apps built into their hardware. Some come with wide-open Internet browsers as well, and that means potential trouble. You have Playboy TV completely blocked. Great. It's a good first step, but what does that really mean when there are millions of free hardcore videos available through our web-enabled TV sets?

Did the preceding paragraph come as a shock? Even if it did, don't worry, you can deal with it. One of the most effective methods you have for controlling the flood of pornography into your home is through a router filter configuration. This is relatively new technology. It is also very simple to use, which is a major point in its favor. Another point in its favor is that the same technology (amazingly) works on all routers. A router filter acts as a safety layer between the pipe entering the house and all of the devices inside the house. Its function is to stop unwanted content *before* it is pumped into your home, and it is very adept at doing that. In a way, a router filter is sort of like the moat we spoke about earlier: it keeps the enemy from entering from every possible angle, which means it works equally well in regard to both Internet filtering and TV/movie/cable filtering, so that sneaky computer masquerading as a TV in order to lull you into a false sense of security is no longer a problem ... and neither are all those many and varied browsers scattered around on your various electronic devices.

Router filters also serve another more subtle function: they turn the rules you've agreed on regarding the Internet and sexually explicit material from theory into reality, and that's a very good thing. The router filter makes clear to all the residents of your home as well as to your guests exactly what your media standards are. It completely disallows content that you and your spouse have deemed objectionable, and in so doing it draws a very visible line in the sand, so to speak. In other words, router filters are a bold, broad, and highly visible statement to anyone who accesses your network. They're like a big, burly cop standing in front of you as you drive down a long road, his hand raised, saying: "This far and not one inch farther!"

But here's a reality check: a router filter is a tool that will protect you in many ways, but there will always be loopholes. For example, what about someone — a friend of your child, for example — who brings his own device into your home? While the router filter is good for home computers, it is *not* able to protect a visitor with a smartphone from accessing the Internet (and thereby pornography) from their own phone.

Digital devices are so portable these days, and adolescents are so prone to have large numbers of friends and acquaintances (each with his own transportable technology in his backpack or pocket) coming and going at all times, that this is a very real concern. You may not be aware of it the instant someone tries to use your network to access porn on *his* devices; in fact, you may not even be home at that moment. Sadly, problems like this have become extremely common and only underscore the importance of several points we have already discussed, such as equipping your kids to resist porn from within themselves and knowing your kids' friends and their families.

In addition to router filtering, Internet monitoring and filtering software are great tools to add to a home defense plan. Unlike router blockers, which monitor an entire network, these are software products that monitor and protect individual devices. This type of software acts as a filter between each device and the router itself rather than the router and the outside world. No technology is perfect, just as no person is perfect; therefore, it's possible that something objectionable might make it past the first filter into your home. So, you have to have this second line of defense.

Even if some objectionable material made it past the router filter into your pipeline, the type of monitoring software I'm talking about will probably be able to neutralize it. In other words, it will prevent it from being accessible to your phones or tablets. As with any software, this has its limits. Some porn sites now use a code which blocks the blocker, a very disturbing development. Another limitation involves some Google searches for images and videos. The video itself will be blocked but the searcher *may* be allowed to see review pictures or thumbnails of illicit images.

Again, nothing's perfect, and we shouldn't allow any protective software to give us a false sense of invulnerability, but with the two-pronged approach I've just described, you will be able to achieve a wide moat and a substantial amount of protection.

Digital Assistance

I cannot recommend strongly enough that preteen children should have this blocking software on their devices as well as any device to which they regularly have access. As far as I can see, not to install such safeguards when your kids are young and clueless is to stray perilously close to being a neglectful parent — and I mean that in the most literal of terms.

It may surprise you to learn, however, that I also recommend that parents should slowly allow for *less blocking* in "tween" years. Step by step you should move from the world of *blocking* software to that of *accountability* software for your teens. This software allows access to virtually everything on the Internet but tracks all activity and reports back to a designated partner. Of course, "designated partner" means you. Obviously, this can by dicey, and there's a real element of danger in it. But *all* of life involves danger, so we just accept that, trust God, and do our best.

An essential part of being a parent is to acknowledge that our daughters and sons are maturing and are becoming capable of acting more responsibly and thoughtfully than they did as small children.

Clearly, this transition ought to be accomplished slowly and carefully, and the timing will vary with every child. It should be accomplished nonetheless. Why? Because as a parent you have many responsibilities; one of the greatest is to protect your children from harm. Another that is just as great is to allow your children to grow into the adults they are meant to become. At times these two responsibilities seem to force us to work at cross purposes, and porn is likely to present us with one of those times. When parents confront something as evil and potentially damaging as porn, we have a strong tendency to allow our love to transform itself into a smothering overprotectiveness without even realizing that it has done so. This is something we must guard against. An essential part of being a parent is to acknowledge that our daughters and sons are maturing and are becoming capable of acting more responsibly and thoughtfully than they did as small children.

I know it's hard to return your defending sword to its scabbard, step aside, and watch the child you once held in your arms walk alone into a world that is dangerous and damaging. But that is a moment that must come for us all. If you have taught your child well, if you have given him a solid foundation in his faith, if you have shown both by your instruction and your life what purity is and why it is of great importance, this transition from blocking to account-ability software should be manageable with software such as that provided by Covenant Eyes. It will demonstrate to your child that you are aware he is growing up and that you trust him. It will probably make him want to strive to be worthy of that trust. It will also allow for important conversations when the child veers off into problem territory — and he will veer, for he's an adolescent. Don't panic: one or two isolated mistakes do not a porn addict make — if you deal with them properly.

You must confront such indiscretions directly but with compassion, remembering how you felt when you were your child's age and the temptations to which you were subject. Of course, you will be walking a delicate balance, and you will be dealing with the huge obstacle of adolescent em-barrassment and shame. Nothing can bring that embarrass-ment to the forefront like a parent who exposes his child's "secret" activities on the Internet in a ham-handed and in-sensitive way. However, if you have played your cards right, you will have arrived at a moment that can lead to increased trust and closeness. It's frightening and difficult but well worth the effort. I am quite certain that if you have had those talks about sexuality that we recommended earlier in this book, things will go relatively easily, and everyone will survive nicely (even you!).

You can employ a third layer of defense by configur-ing devices individually. We will not go into technical steps in this book, but you should know that every smartphone or portable device includes parental control options. You should also know that smartphones present an enormous problem. According to the Barna Research Group's study of teen Internet use in 2014, 80 percent of an adolescent's contact with pornography is achieved through smartphones. While these devices have added to our lives in terms of functionality and access, they have taken a great deal from us by enabling us to carry porn in our pockets at virtually every moment of our lives.

I must reluctantly admit that despite the potential for danger, you are unlikely to be able to eliminate cell phones from even a young child's life. Parents should be keenly aware of the peer pressure their children are under regarding such devices. They are status symbols and have become so socially important that many educators have stopped trying to prohibit kids from bringing them to school and now concentrate their efforts on simply *managing* cell phone usage during class. Every child will desperately want a phone and will hound you to death until you give him one. This presents real challenges as you attempt to form and shape your children in the image of Christ, but with a few simple countermeasures, you can still tilt the scales in your favor.

Digital Functionality Oversight

The best solution for helping kids handle the power they carry in their pockets is by using what I call "the graduated method." If your ten-year-old, for instance, has a phone, it should be one that allows texting and phone calls and absolutely nothing else — no camera. There should be no other apps on his phone at all. A thirteen-year-old, on the other hand, might have several social media apps but only those that her parents have permitted her to download. Don't take chances: keep the ID number needed to complete the download and don't share it with your child. This process gives parents an opportunity to put an extra layer of protection in place: you have limited your child's apps to those you have already previewed while permitting her to develop a sense of independence. For that you deserve a pat on the back.

When you feel your child is ready for a smartphone, you can take the following approach. While you're at your local electronics store dubiously purchasing him his first smartphone, here's what you do to banish the doom-laden thoughts that started afflicting you the instant the device was placed in his eager hand: take a few minutes to have the store's tech support staff teach you how to set parental controls on the device. It's not tricky, but you don't want to assume you've got everything locked down when you haven't. Once you get that information, you'll be more-or-less in control of things and won't have to spend nearly as much time wondering if hara-kiri is really the only honorable option left to you considering what you've just allowed to come into your child's possession.

Now you can easily set up passwords to prevent your son or daughter (or their friends) from changing the control settings on phones and other devices, including the addition or deletion of new apps, and the alteration of security settings. This is vitally important for devices we give to young children but also very important for devices that are in the hands of older kids. Perhaps the biggest advantage of this tool is its ability to turn off the setting that allows the user to delete his Internet browsing history. This is invaluable, as the browsing history (which you will examine regularly) will reveal any porn searches your child has attempted. If you study it carefully, you will discover that it's also pretty good at giving indications as to whether an apparent porn search was intentional or just the result of some naïve and probably innocent mistakes made as your child was hunting for some reasonable bit of information. Of course, you'll want to deal with those two possibilities in very different ways.

If you are unfamiliar with how to prevent deletions of browsing history on your kids' phones, don't worry. Simply Google the words "how to delete browsing history" and you'll be an expert within minutes.

One final point — a slightly touchy point regarding parental browsing histories: a willingness to prevent the deletion of your own history as well as having accountability software on the father's computer and cell phone is essential for couples who are serious about building a united front yet have themselves had a problem with Internet porn. A husband who has been addicted to porn or has at least accessed Internet porn, no matter how frequently or infrequently, is always going to seem to his wife like a vaguely untrustworthy partner in this enterprise. It is possible to give her peace of mind and also make her aware that you are completely behind the no-porn policy of your household by surrendering the capacity to delete your own browsing history and to use protective software.

This may seem a small step, but it's a significant one. It removes those lingering doubts, that uncertainty about whether it is truly possible to trust, and can even strengthen your marriage. So now you've got it. Each device is password protected; each device has parental controls set by you and in your favor; each device has monitoring software; and the pipe coming into your home has a filter on it to keep the sludge from entering at all. So you're in great shape. Your moat is so wide that you need binoculars just to see land on the other side of it. Right?

Well ... perhaps. Even if you're perfectly safe at the moment, your invulnerability may be more short lived than you'd hoped, for technology is an endlessly shifting landscape. If you stand still for a moment, everything changes around you, and that disturbing fact is what we'll be discussing in a couple of chapters.

Porn Channels Checklist

Before we end this chapter, I thought I'd give you a handy little checklist to help you dig that moat and porn-proof your home as much as possible. It'll help. I guarantee it.

- ❑ Mobile devices: Put filter software on your mobile phones, tablets, and iPods.

- ❑ YouTube and videos: Put "AdBlock Plus" on your devices. "Covenant Eyes" also monitors the titles of YouTube videos.

- ❑ Shopping catalogs: Many catalogs use soft porn to sell. Consider "41 pounds" to stop them.

- ❑ DVDs: Prescreen and throw out any "bonus" discs or inappropriate content.

- ❑ Netflix, Hulu Plus, etc.: Consider dropping cable or unsubscribe these services or use parental controls.

- ❑ TV commercials: Consider subscribing to a TV recording device and skipping commercials entirely.

- ❑ Kid's friends: Ensure your kids are well grounded in anti-porn information. Also, watch social media issues, an enormous source of inappropriate content, and "sharing."

- ❑ Mobile game ads: Use ad-blocking software. For mobile devices, put in "airplane mode."

- ❑ Music and cover art: Be vigilant in selecting good music as well as the graphics that appear. Thumbs down any music or art that contains unsuitable lyrics or artwork.

- ❑ Video games: Heed the ESRB rating system. Even E-10 ratings should be previewed by a parent.

❑ Books: Read reviews of all children's books before allowing them. Also, review book cover art.

❑ Apps: SnapChat, Gaggle, and more. Institute public passwords so you know them all. Consider "KytePhone" for time limits and more.

PARENTS' PERSONAL REFLECTIONS

- On a scale of 1 to 10, how would you rate your home's defensive posture against all porn exposure?

- What is the greatest threat to your family within the home concerning pornography?

- How many personal digital devices do you have in your home? Are they all protected? In what ways?

GROUP DISCUSSION

- Discuss the challenges some parents feel about "spying" on their children's digital activity.

- Discuss the difficulties in eliminating or significantly reducing sources of pornography (mobile phones, cable, internet, and so forth).

- Discuss how the rapid pace of technology affects your ability to protect your family and consider ways to stay on top of at least some of that rapid development.

ACTION STEPS

- Destroy (not just throw out) every piece of inappropriate sexual media in your home.

- Implement digital protection strategy steps.

- Begin checking your children's social website accounts for any inappropriate comments and actions.

- Remove all computers from private rooms and place in a public room in your home.

RESOURCES

See the filtering technologies, accountability software, malware blocking systems, and home blocking systems listed in appendix A. Also take a look at the Secure Mama blog (www.securemama.com).

CHAPTER 8

FIFTH STRATEGY

ENACT FULL-SCOPE LEADERSHIP

So now you've got a few tools — and they're good ones — that will help you in your battle with pornography. But if you're going to become the kind of leader who can fight that battle effectively, you've got to be very clear on exactly who and what you're up against and who your allies are.

So let's take a look.

We've already spoken often about *hardcore* pornography — porn at its most barbaric and damaging. That, of course, is your primary opponent, but keep in mind the almost ubiquitous presence of porn in its "softer," more socially acceptable forms — the slow but steady "pornification" of our culture that has occurred over the past few decades.

It's a fatal error to buy into the idea that this soft porn fed us by the modern media is acceptable. It is insidious and toxic, for it deadens the soul, preparing the way for its more hateful and violent sibling.

There are literally countless examples of the pornification of culture that I could mention, but I'm going to select a very familiar one. In fact, I bet some of you have actually contributed a few dollars of your hard-earned money to its astonishing success (if so, you should think long and hard about that). It's a novel, and later a movie, called *Fifty Shades of Grey*, the first installment in a trilogy of novels dealing with the same characters and themes. Those themes, by the way, go by names such as: sadomasochism, bondage and discipline, domination and submission. These are not "soft" porn themes, generally, but the manner in which these books have slid into the culture and been deemed acceptable illustrates the pornification of which I speak.

Fifty Shades of Grey is a lousy piece of writing but a masterful move in the culture wars, for it has been extraordinarily effective in expanding the normalization of porn, especially among a group that is not as easily drawn into the pornographic world. That group is comprised of women and girls, and it probably includes people you love.

Typically, women are not as attracted to pornographic images as are men. Many women, however, can be drawn to stories involving intense relationships, especially romantic ones. *Fifty Shades of Grey* capitalizes on this brilliantly by cocooning its tale of the sadomasochistic submission of a very young woman to a rich and powerful older man in the forms and conventions of a traditional romance novel (the sort of thing pioneered in the nineteenth century by the Brontë sisters and commercialized — to great and enduring success — by Harlequin Romances).

All the standard elements of the typical romance novel are neatly and cleverly in place in *Fifty Shades of Grey*, signaling to the reader that she is simply reading another example of a genre that she knows well and that is completely culturally acceptable. Ultimately, however, *Fifty Shades of Grey* is not an example of the romance genre in any traditional sense but is simply parasitic on it, replacing love and enduring relationship (the goal of every romance novel) with aberrant sexuality and the abject and graphic sexual submission of a woman to a man — a man who in more rational times would be considered a dangerous deviant, an evil character to be overcome by the hero of the novel, rather than himself being the hero.

Fifty Shades of Grey, by the way, did not just spring magically onto the scene with no precedents or pedigree. It would probably never have been possible without the slow but steady "porn creep" that has occurred in the romance genre over several decades. Before 1980, it was a given in such novels that the heroine would be chaste and remain a virgin until her wedding night. In the 1980s, the heroine was permitted to have a limited and vague sexual history, and she was allowed to sleep with the hero toward the end of the book, but only after they had declared their intent to marry. Soon, however, sexual scenes began to multiply in number and increase in intensity; they also began to occur before the characters were in any type of committed relationship.

Eventually, tradition and good taste were simply thrown to the wind. This can be shown most succinctly by advice a budding romance writer once received from an editor at a major publishing house. Here it is verbatim: "It's all right if the heroine is raped, but only by the hero, and he should regret it, at least by the end of the book." In that rather bizarre advice, we see not just the first step toward *Fifty Shades of Grey* but a huge step taken in the normalization of porn — not to mention a type of porn that deals with violence and submission — for that most difficult of all porn markets: women.

What are you as a leader in your family going to do about the intrusion of pornography into your family's life in culturally sanctioned forms such as *Fifty Shades of Grey*?

Everyday Challenge

As a leader in your family, what are you going to do about the intrusion of pornography into your family's life in culturally sanctioned forms such as *Fifty Shades of Grey?* Simply modifying your computer helps, but it is not going to completely meet the need in this regard. Novels are far from the only source of "soft" porn in our lives and the lives of our children. You've also got to consider movies that graphically and positively portray seduction, promiscuity, and infidelity; music lyrics and videos that are simply foul; mainstream magazines touting not just sexual "freedom" but sexual techniques; and, of course, the ever-popular social media sites that seem to be in the business of slowly desensitizing young people to sexual exploitation as the sites promote skewed visions of love, intimacy, and personal dignity.

The first thing you must do if you expect to deal with the soft porn explosion is surrender your illusions. You have to accept that this is in the very air we breathe. Mainstream fiction and other forms of mainstream media can no longer be assumed to be harmless. You and your spouse are going to have to stay abreast of what is being published, what is being televised, and what comes streaming into your home through various forms of technology. This is an essential part of digging that moat!

Allies

This is a big job for one or two people. Therefore, I suggest working closely with like-minded parents who are confronting the same issues. You can find them at your child's school or at your parish or in your diocese. Other religious institutions can also be a great resource. Try to get an informal group up and running (you're a leader, after all), and remember that there's strength in numbers. If you form a team that is on the lookout for these softcore porn home invasions — a little intelligence-gathering-and-sharing group — you will be able to accomplish quite a bit in protecting your family.

Consider forming such a subgroup in your parent-teacher organization. You can find useful parent education videos for your group to view at www.cmgparent.org. These include eleven short videos about parental controls on iOS, Kindle Fire, Chromebook, Netflix, Google safe search, You-Tube safe search, Instagram, and more.

The local library is also a potential collaborator in this. Part of a librarian's job is to know what is appropriate in the way of reading material for children and adolescents and what is not. Libraries now also deal regularly with digital sources of information and entertainment, so that's helpful, too. Find a librarian who is sympathetic to your cause and pick her brain ruthlessly. Don't worry, she won't mind.

At the risk of seeming redundant I must also recommend another of those talks with your kids. When a phenomenon like *Fifty Shades of Grey* comes along, they'll be very aware of it (probably before you are), and they'll be fascinated. Many of their friends will be immersed in it. In some adolescent groups, carrying around such a book may even become a status symbol. Don't let those groups of kids steal your leadership from you. Make a preemptive strike and explain in very unambiguous terms what is wrong with novels that stray into pornography. Point out their dehumanizing features, their excursions into activities that have been judged sick and perverted by most cultures.

Explain how such a book is opposed to your faith and your understanding of the dignity and holiness of each human being. Perhaps a mother might want to find a relationship-oriented novel of real literary quality and read it with her daughter, emphasizing whenever possible the uplifting characteristics of that book as opposed to the degrading characteristics of the one that slithered to the top of the best-seller list.

I wanted to discuss *Fifty Shades of Grey* for several reasons, but one of the most important is that it is different from the majority of porn in that it is written primarily for women and girls. In the battle against porn, we almost reflexively assume that our sons are the ones we must protect in the most aggressive way possible. We are only too aware that they are easy targets for pornographers — sitting ducks, really. Often we almost forget about our daughters, thinking they are more likely to be repulsed by porn than seduced by it. But scores of pornographic websites cater to young and older women. By women, for women is their claim. Most parents believe their daughters would never visit such sites. Many parents would be wrong.

If *Fifty Shades of Grey* proved anything, it proved that if pornography is packaged in the right way, it can be made appealing to women, seduce them as easily as it can seduce men, and act as a gateway to hardcore pornography use. The author and publishers of *Fifty Shades of Grey* played their cards perfectly. Women of a very wide range of ages read the book by the millions. Over one hundred million copies were sold globally in a short time with nearly fifty million of those being sold in the United States alone. It quickly became the fastest selling fiction publication in the history of its publisher, Random House (one of our most prestigious publishing houses). It has been called "mommy-porn," and I must say that I can't think of a more fitting or sadder epithet.

Fifty Shades of Grey is not the only foray porn is trying to make into the lives of women. A porn site aimed specifically at women offers the following enticement on its website: "If you like to read your porn instead of watching it or don't want your neighbors hearing the stars of the video screaming in ecstasy, then this site has you covered. The writing is high caliber, racy, and seriously sexy. Plus, it's free." Another porn site with its eye on women says: "Our favorite thing? The audio stories. Original erotic literature read to you by a man in a very sensual voice."

So no heads in the sand, please! Our daughters are at risk. With the porn industry's vast sweep and determination, we must never assume that girls are safe simply because they aren't glued to a computer screen at three in the morning. Porn's approach to women and girls can be different and subtler than the one it uses to hook men and boys, but it will be as determined and relentless.

In *Fifty Shades of Grey* it is the young woman who submits to degradation and it is the man who utterly controls her.... No amount of added romanticism can conceal the bleak fact that women are the victims of porn.

When you combine the seduction of a romanticized version of porn with the well-known "hookup" culture of hit-and-run sexual encounters, something our culture tolerates and possibly even approves of, I think we can see a formula for despair in the making. Both combine to leave young women with a diminished attitude toward relationships, men, and themselves. Like porn in all its myriad forms, it leads only to disappointment and emptiness. In the case of a young woman, however, it can lead to something else: her exploitation by men, her transformation in their eyes from a person to an object who provides pleasure, and her willing acceptance of that transformation. No matter how it is romanticized by its purveyors, porn remains a deadly example of the misuse of women by men. Remember: In *Fifty Shades of Grey* it is the young woman who submits to degradation and it is the man who utterly controls her. This is the message that porn conveys to our daughters. No amount of added romanticism can conceal the bleak fact that women are the victims of porn.

The problem of young women and pornography has grown to the extent that organizations now exist to help porn-addicted women — Dirty Girl Ministries is one such organization, and it can be reached through its website. I hope you don't ever have to use it, but tuck that information away and pray you will never need it.

Occupied Territory

I said earlier in this chapter that we must know what and whom we're up against, and I meant it. So far we've learned that we're up against a voracious and surprisingly creative porn industry that is capable of adapting its tactics to hook different types of people — no one's off limits. We also learned we're up against a culture that normalizes porn a little more each day. These are formidable opponents. But they're only part of the package because, as C.S. Lewis once said, "We live in enemy-occupied territory."

The enemy, of course, is Satan. Many people today — and you may be among them — do not accept that the devil is a real entity with personal attributes, who is committed to our destruction and to keeping us from true happiness and a holy relationship with God. So I'm going to present some quotes that will drive home the point both of his existence and of the reality of spiritual warfare. Please read these over when you have time to pause and let the truth of the words enter your heart and motivate your actions. Here we go.

To the discomfort of many of his admirers, especially within the secular sphere, Pope Francis often speaks about the reality of the devil. On various occasions he has said:

> "Maybe his [Satan's] greatest achievement in these times has been to make us believe that he does not exist, and that all can be fixed on a purely human level."

> "The devil is always crouching at our door, in front of our heart, and wants to come in."

> "On this point, there are no nuances. There is a battle and a battle where salvation is at play, eternal salvation."

> "The devil also exists in the twenty-first century, and we need to learn from the Gospel how to battle against him."

Scripture backs him up. St. Peter wrote: "Your opponent the devil is prowling around like a roaring lion looking for [someone] to devour" (1 Peter 5:8) — words that have particular relevance to the issue of pornography. Have you ever watched a television program that highlighted the lives of lions in the wilds of Africa? One fact that always emerges in these presentations is this: when hunting for prey, a lion generally stalks one of three types of victims: an animal who is wounded; one that is very young; or one that is alone, separated from the herd.

The application to porn is obvious. Its most easily tackled prey generally consists of the young and unformed who don't really grasp what they're getting themselves into; those who are emotionally or spiritually wounded, which includes many of us but especially those who have known little love or believe they are not worthy of love and so live their lives perched on the edge of despair; and those who are cut off from others or who are estranged from God and no longer part of the community of God, the Church.

I have always been taken with Dante's striking and unusual portrayal of Satan in *The Inferno*, and I think the image he used can tell us a lot about the strengths and (more importantly) the weaknesses of pornography. For Dante, Satan is no fiery demon of unimaginable power. He is an immobile creature, encased in ice up to his chest. He cannot move because the ice is too strong and too dense. Yet this devil's prison is of his own making. It is the result of the furious beating of his reptilian wings which generates a wind so frigid that it keeps the ice frozen and unbreakable. At the depths of Dante's vision of hell, every bit of warmth has been banished. Infinite cold is all that exists.

The warmth of real love and forgiveness,
of true community, and the strong bonds of
family life can work to melt the frozen unreality
of pornography.

From a spiritual point of view perhaps we could call pornography a frozen unreality. It offers us a world that seems enticing on the surface, but it is a world without a shred of warmth — a world that is frigidly closed and imprisoned. The warmth of real love and forgiveness, of true community, and the strong bonds of family life can work to melt the frozen unreality of pornography.

A few more quotes and we're done — I think by now you get the point.

Scripture tells us that "our struggle is not with flesh and blood but with the principalities, with the powers ... with the evil spirits in the heavens. Therefore, put on the armor of God that you may be able to resist in the evil day, and, having done everything, to hold your ground" (Ephesians 6:12–13). We need to be equipped intellectually, physically, and spiritually, praying with our spouse and children, and over our children. "Resist the devil, and he will flee from you" (James 4:7). These are very hopeful — even joyful — words! If we fight him, the devil will back off — but we must fight him and teach our children to recognize his ways and to fight him as well. Pope St. John Paul II said it this way: "'Spiritual combat' is another element of life which needs to be taught anew and proposed once more to all Christians today. It is a secret and interior art, an invisible struggle in which [we] engage every day against the temptations, the evil suggestions that the demon tries to plant in our hearts" (Address, May 25, 2002).

As you fight against a spiritual reality that wishes to drain the warmth from your life, and with it everything you cherish, you need powerful allies in that fight. You can find the most powerful ally of all if you take time to sit quietly and pray as best you can before the Blessed Sacrament. It is there you will find strength for the journey to purity and there that you will find victory.

PARENTS' PERSONAL REFLECTIONS

- What material have you read or seen that our culture tells us is harmless but which includes some pornographic elements? What attracted you to it? Did you have any moral qualms at the time?

- What is your attitude toward material that once would have been understood to be pornographic but now is considered harmless? Do you agree with the culture or with the Church on this matter?

- How do you imagine the Devil? In Hebrew, the word "satan" means adversary. Does that word help you to better understand the objective reality of evil?

GROUP DISCUSSION

- How has our culture become too accepting of what was, not long ago, considered sexually immoral?

- How do you, as parents, challenge or discuss with your children their media choices?

- Does pushing back on sexually explicit entertainment, fashion, language, etc., make you feel "prudish"?

ACTION STEPS

- Discuss with your children the alleged differences between hardcore pornography and the softcore type of pornography that is available at your local bookstore.

- Pornography ensnares both men and women. Given this, consider specific ways you can protect your daughter as well as your sons.

- Read the sections of the *Catechism* that relate to the Devil. Discuss what you think of them. Be honest about whether or not you believe in an actual personality behind evil. Utilize this reality to encourage your commitment to protecting your children and family.

RESOURCES

How to Win the Culture War, Peter Kreeft, IVP Books.
Manual for Spiritual Warfare, Paul Thigpen, TAN Books.

CHAPTER 9

SIXTH STRATEGY

RULES AND BOUNDARIES — FOUNDATION FOR FREEDOM

We've already touched on freedom and the threats that pornography poses to true liberty. In this chapter, we're going to look again at the idea of freedom, but with an eye to setting legitimate and productive boundaries to allow us to build our sexual integrity.

Setting boundaries to freedom? That sounds un-American. We all love our freedom and resist restrictions that prevent us from doing what we really want to do. In other words, we don't care very much for rules, which seem to us like unjust impositions. Is that simply part of human nature? Probably, but for us twenty-first-century Americans it may be more than that. The idea of freedom has become very much a part of our self-understanding. We demand it and decry whatever may limit it. In some ways, we've made an idol of it.

Real freedom is acting in accord with the will
of God, for that is the same as acting in accord
with our most essential nature.

But if we see with Catholic eyes, we know that freedom or liberty comes not from giving into our whims and fancies — for ultimately that becomes a certain type of bondage. Real freedom is acting in accord with the will of God, for that is the same as acting in accord with our most essential nature.

To you, as parents, falls the less-than-congenial task of establishing rules and boundaries for your children. Make no mistake about it: those rules will limit their freedom in certain ways, but they will expand it in far more important ways. If you're anything like me, something deep within you is reluctant to do that. You and I are as much a product of our times as anyone else, and influenced by the anarchic freedom prized by our culture.

But I want you to create a far better thing: a life that includes definite rules and boundaries that flow directly from love, a life that prizes relationships and is capable of holiness.

Setting Standards

So let's just go straight for the rules that will help to do that. These have stood the test of time and have helped protect many from the world of pornography. I offer them to you as a starting point, a way to establish boundaries that are clear to everyone and a way to enhance your relationship with those you love.

Example Rule 1: There is to be no Internet use by anyone in our household after _____ p.m.

With the rare exception of a test or work deadline, there really is no reason for any home to have a device on the Internet after about 10 p.m. For kids, all connections to the Internet should end a minimum of an hour before bedtime. First of all, kids need time to decompress, to leave the cyber world and reenter the real world — to reconnect with those flesh-and-blood beings (that means you, your spouse, and their siblings) who are important in their lives. In other words, the last thing they see before turning out the light should be your loving smile, not a zombie skull exploding on their computer screen.

By the way, the same goes for dad. Many men find the "after-hours" browsing the most dangerous of all times to be enticed to view pornography. Disconnect as early as possible. Try a good book instead, or better yet, try a conversation with your spouse.

Example Rule 2: There is never to be any Internet use in any room of our house if the door to that room is closed.

Here's a fact: temptation will aggressively seek us out, even if we live in houses with well-monitored systems. So let's do what we can to avoid the temptation in the first place. There are countless websites that are really soft porn sites; there are many more that are not considered pornographic but still are more than erotic enough to get things rolling. They might not do the kind of damage that hardcore sites are capable of, but they open a metaphorical door that is best kept closed.

So let's keep the physical door open in an effort to avoid the problem. An open door and a few lights turned on often are more than enough to prevent a temptation from getting the better of us. Leaving doors open to rooms where the Internet is being accessed tells everyone in the house that nothing is being hidden. Let's face it: temptation is always more easily resisted when you know that giving in to it can lead to unpleasant results.

Example Rule 3: Internet sessions are limited to _____ minutes per sitting and _____ total minutes per day. (This rule also applies to video games.)

How many couples do we know whose lives at night seem to be reduced to watching TV side by side with both laptops open and a cell phone or two in play? Do I need to tell you that children learn from watching you that this is an appropriate way to live? Probably not.

Do I need to tell you that human relationships suffer or at least take a backseat when everybody's plugged into cyberspace 24/7? I don't think so.

What you and your family must do as a group is to figure out the best method for keeping track of technology minutes, establish a daily limit that doesn't send anybody into shock, and then live by it. Real relationships require face-to-face time, and just in case you're wondering, digital messaging doesn't count even if you add those smiley faces to your messages.

Example Rule 4: There is to be no Internet use after more than two drinks of alcohol.

Yes, this one applies to adults rather than your fifth grader, but it's still important, for we're all more vulnerable than we like to believe. Alcohol is a well-known pornography catalyst. Alcohol limits inhibitions and produces greater risk-taking behavior. Anyone in your home who combines drinking and a lot of time on the Internet is in a potentially serious situation.

Example Rule 5: There are to be no digital devices in a kid's room overnight, especially if he has friends spending the night with him.

Of course, I didn't have to include this one because you understand the situation very well by now — but you can never be too safe. Everything stated above applies here. An overnight with a bunch of adolescent boys can be turned into a disaster by one undiscovered smartphone, so be on the alert. I'm not advocating strip searches, but I am warning you (as if I need to) that kids are very inventive when it comes to concealing things from adults. Just consider yourself forewarned.

Even if pornography is not a problem in a particular situation, this rule should still be enforced.

When we insist that all devices go to a central location to charge overnight, we sever any disordered attachments that may exist as well as decrease the chances that our kids will outsmart the parental controls we've so carefully instituted.

Example Rule 6: There will be no deleting browsing history.

I know we've been here before, but it's a place worth revisiting. All electronic transmissions leave a trace, and web browsers are no exception. When this rule is employed, all parties understand that any device is open for inspection and accountability at all times. It may seem at times like a scare tactic in that it threatens the sudden exposure of secret things. But it is so effective in keeping teenagers on the straight and narrow that its benefits far outweigh anything else. This is a must.

Example Rule 7: There will be designated "no-screen" periods in our household.

This rule is a favorite for most adults, but I must warn you that it is utterly despised by kids. The family as a whole decides on a certain day or most of a day each week during which nobody is electronically connected to anything. A word of advice regarding this: you may need to reassure your children that they will survive such periods and that nobody in the entire history of the world has ever died from Internet Deprivation Syndrome no matter what their friends tell them.

I strongly suggest that the best no-screen day for most families is Sunday, as that would help us "keep holy the Lord's day," which is something we're not nearly as good at as we once were. Whatever day you choose, instituting a no-screen day will involve a small sacrifice; it will also produce many graces. Not only does it reclaim precious family time together, but it contradicts what the world proclaims to be normal but which we know is not. Try it for three weeks and see what happens. I suspect that in that time you'll begin to reap real benefits in terms of strengthening family relationships.

But … if nixing an entire day is too challenging to start with, you might begin by enforcing a ban on smaller periods of time. If you go this route, you must be especially careful to make that time meaningful and not just boring downtime for your kids. Plan some physical activities that will be enjoyed by the whole family. Make sure there's as much face-to-face conversation as possible. Games, good reading, and other activities of the sort that have enriched countless lives (until we gave them up to play on our computers) are other good choices.

Use your imagination. There are literally countless possibilities from which to choose. You might even convince your children that real life is more interesting than virtual life. If you manage that one, you have achieved a victory beyond price.

Rule 8: The ten-second rule.

This is vital. It's a rule meant to encourage your children to report to you immediately (within ten seconds if possible) any scary, dangerous, or sexualized encounter they may have on any digital device. Obviously, you must discuss this one with your kids carefully and with great sensitivity. You don't want to frighten them. As a corollary to this, you also want to talk to them concerning any information about themselves they make available to others online.

The daughter of a friend of mine very innocently posted a picture of her college dorm room early in her freshman year. She was proud of her interior-decorating skills and wanted to show them off. Unfortunately, she also wanted to show how perfectly her new sheets matched the walls, and to do this she turned the bed down. This was the picture she posted on her social media page — which, not surprisingly, was seen as an invitation to a sexual encounter.

I can hear you gasping in horror, but the story is a reminder to parents that our children, who are so sophisticated in many ways, are still innocent in others.

Speak to them gently but firmly and help them avoid such problems, and make sure they will bring their concerns to you in as close to ten seconds as is humanly possible.

Example Rule 9: Gaming.

No gaming is allowed that involves sexual themes, costumes, actions, or language. In addition, excessive violence — especially against women — is strictly prohibited. The problem with gaming also includes the "training" of participants in an ever-increasing need for speed and instant gratification. This has serious implications for brain development in addition to inappropriate content.

Sacraments are the normal means by which we receive God's life, assistance, and love.
As a family, it is important to commit to a regular routine of going to confession.

Example Rule 10: Embrace the sacraments.

Sacraments are the normal means by which we receive God's life, assistance, and love. As a family, it is important to commit to a regular routine of going to confession, confessing sinful thoughts, words, and actions of a sexual nature. This is most effectively adhered to when a family goes to reconciliation together. The witness of parents to their children is invaluable, and the experience results in our receiving additional sacramental grace to help us in our battles against sexual sin. It also reminds all family members of the unconditional love God has for each of us. Further, it reinforces the need for accountability and humility while working against a sense of shame and despair.

Obviously, attendance at Mass on a weekly basis — again, as a family — is an opportunity to reinforce your commitment to Christ and to be strengthened through the power of the Holy Spirit against succumbing to sexual temptation.

Other beneficial activities include daily prayer, occasional fasting as a family, and a regular family devotion such as the rosary or Eucharistic adoration.

Benefits of Boundaries

So now we've got a few rules that can help you establish reasonable boundaries. Of course you should feel free to modify them in ways that will work best for your particular situation and your particular family. But before we move on to something else, I'd like to share some guidelines that my friend Pastor Darrell Brazell offers in his workbook, *New Hope for Recovery from Sexual Addiction.*

Better safe than sorry. First of all, when it comes to dealing with porn, it's always better to be safe than sorry.

What does that mean? It means that when establishing rules and boundaries, you should probably start off being stricter and more vigilant than you think you need to be. The adolescent personality is a challenge, to say the least. Many of our kids crave excitement; they want to live on the edge, although they generally have no clue what that "edge" really is or means. They have been taught well by our society to worship freedom, especially their own, and they have also been taught that freedom means a lack of all restrictions rather than acting in a way that accords with their real nature. Add all this together, and you can see the potential for both problems and conflict.

Many times, parents will say something like this: "I'll start with a very loose and ill-defined boundary. If that doesn't work and my kids crash, I'll gradually tighten things until I get it exactly right."

The problem with this approach is that it presupposes a crash, something that may take time and real effort to recover from — something that might cause terrible damage. What if there are several crashes before you get everything fine-tuned? What does that do to your kids — to your family? Your goal is to protect your kids consistently and to the best of your ability, not to find out through trial and error exactly how much resistance they have or don't have. (A clue: They don't have much at all. That's the reason we need these rules and boundaries to begin with!)

The opposite approach may seem strict, but it works much better. Start with tight and well-established boundaries, and then when your kids prove themselves capable of operating well within them, gradually (very, very gradually) loosen them.

Boundaries don't work unless they are firm and
consistent. Never change a boundary without
a great deal of thought.

Better firm than flimsy. Another bit of advice from
Pastor Brazell is that boundaries don't work unless they are
firm and consistent. Never change a boundary without a
great deal of thought. If a boundary can be changed whenever your child requests it, it isn't a real boundary, and it's
probably useless. Yes, your kids will beg and plead and
wheedle. They'll also sulk and pout and accuse you of being the most heartless parent in the history of parenthood,
including those characters from Greek mythology who ate
their own children. Big deal. Nobody ever said being a parent was going to be a piece of cake. Stand firm and wait
awhile; they'll get over it.

Before you change any rule or move any boundary, give
it at least twenty-four hours of consideration. You also must
discuss it with your spouse. If your children see one parent
unilaterally changing rules that both parents established,
you'll be hard pressed to maintain consistency. They'll play
one parent off the other to get what they want, and that's
never good. You must maintain a consistently united front.

Family boundaries. It is important that boundaries
be observed by the entire family. Such common boundaries
eliminate feelings of being personally imposed upon, since
everyone is dealing with exactly the same rule in exactly the
same way. By making all boundaries common ones, you
have a built-in accountability system between siblings. They
aren't likely to turn into the morality police, but they will be
able to hold each other's feet to the fire a bit should one of
them break family rules.

A means to an end. Remember that external controls are essential, but they are not the sole answer. An endless array of boundaries will not keep kids from attempting to violate those boundaries. You must deal with the root issues — our sinful natures will always try to find ways around the boundaries if the root issues go unhealed.

Internet, social media, and email boundaries. Think of the Internet as a loaded weapon: handled correctly, it can be an effective tool; handled incorrectly, it can be an instrument of spiritual and psychological death. Having an unprotected computer in front of your kids, or failing to prepare your kids for the appropriate use of technology, is like inviting them to play Russian roulette.

Drawing up a long list of restrictions is not the goal. The goal is to draw up restrictions that are life-giving for your family.

In the final analysis, parents must consider what boundaries are best for their marriage and their family. Drawing up a long list of restrictions is not the goal. The goal is to draw up restrictions that are life-giving for your family. In the process, keep in mind various issues such as age, gender, sensitivity, and personality and relax in the knowledge that boundary setting is not a once-and-for-all event. Each child, as he or she grows and changes, will require individualized coaching, mentoring, and encouragement. The boundaries you set now will inevitably change. Don't worry. You can do it — there is room to maneuver in all this.

With God's grace and a shared commitment to protecting your marriage and family, you can open a world of freedom to your children — a world in which people are free to live as they were meant to live and with the human dignity they were meant to possess. This is a world that has become fragile in our time, but it is one that can be protected if we observe the boundaries that enable us to be who we must be.

PARENTS' PERSONAL REFLECTIONS

- Rules are not a substitute for relational parenting. Make sure you know the difference.
- Does it bother you to restrict Internet use for your children?
- Consider your own concept of freedom. Does it match that of the Church?

GROUP DISCUSSION

- Most children respond negatively toward restrictions/ boundaries. How can parents prepare for and overcome that?
- Some boundaries are age-specific. How do you navigate and explain differences in rules for family members?
- Discuss how rules and regulations and boundaries help relationships.
- Discuss how ancillary concerns such as physical, verbal, and emotional boundaries impact a family.

ACTION STEPS

- Jointly decide and establish age-appropriate boundaries about pornography and sexually related issues.
- Develop responses to give your children when they "push back" on some of your rules/boundaries.

RESOURCES

Advice Worth Ignoring: How Tuning Out the Experts Can Make You a Better Parent, Dr. Ray Guarendi, Servant Books.

Discipline that Lasts a Lifetime, Dr. Ray Guarendi, Servant Books.

Raising Good Kids: Back to Family Basics, Dr. Ray Guarendi, Our Sunday Visitor.

Boundaries in Marriage, Henry Cloud and John Townsend, Zondervan.

Part Three

BLUEPRINT FOR ACTION

CHAPTER 10

AGE-BASED CONSIDERATIONS

Now that you've reviewed the general strategies for protecting your family, let's discuss when it's appropriate, in general, to apply these strategies, based on the ages of your children. As leaders you will engage in three primary steps: 1) mentorship or teaching; 2) technology applications; and 3) modeling the message of sexual integrity.

Please remember that these stages and their age designations are meant as a general guideline. Your child might be at a slightly younger or older age when you take particular steps. Ultimately it is up to you, the parent, to decide what and when such measures are applied.

Stage One: Pregnancy

During this time of preparation, consider the following:

- ❑ Reaffirm your own parental commitment to sexual integrity within your marriage.
- ❑ Pray for God's grace in your individual and joint parenting.
- ❑ Have a priest bless your home.
- ❑ If either spouse is struggling with pornography, get help from your priest and Catholic therapist.
- ❑ Destroy (don't just throw out as someone else might find it) any media in the home that is por-

nographic, sexually suggestive, or would not be appropriate for anyone to encounter if they visited your home.

❏ Science has shown that the baby, while still in the womb, begins to understand both the voice and disposition of the mother. Beware of anger, sexually offensive language, and so forth while you are pregnant.

❏ Begin offering daily prayers for your child's spiritual and physical health.

❏ Recommit to a sacramental life as a family.

Stage Two: Infant 0–2 years old

The move from being a couple to being parents is a huge step. Perhaps as no other event can, having a child moves both parents to live for someone other than themselves.

Mentoring

❏ Hold, touch, and speak with great joy and tenderness to your newborn.

❏ Infants begin learning about their bodies through touch.

❏ Nudity is completely asexual to a newborn or young toddler.

❏ Teach your child the real names of body parts such as "penis," "vagina," and "breast." Special words send the wrong message that body part names are "dirty." Clarity is critical.

❏ God created our bodies, and they are beautiful and good.

❑ Engender trust between your child and yourself. This also refers to the home as a trusted environment.

Technology

❑ No child in this age group should *possess* or *have independent access* to *any* digital device.

❑ Media exposure should be limited and only experienced with permission from, and in the presence of, parents.

❑ Begin generally following personal technology development.

❑ *Traditional* media — books, magazines, catalogues, art, and so on — should be monitored for appropriateness and access.

❑ Consider that children in this age group are also frequently in the company of extended family members and friends. Provide strict technology oversight to ensure your child's safety in these additional environments and with these additional individuals as well.

Modeling

❑ Your young child witnesses everything you do and say. Parents need to be discreet in their own sexual behavior and speech.

❑ Positive parental expressions about pregnancy, birth, babies, body image, and family life are critical not only for this age, but also in terms of modeling such expressions for older siblings of the newest child.

❑ The infant/toddler should witness Catholic life pri-
    marily through the sacraments, family and individ-
    ual prayer, and even works of mercy toward others.
    All of these give a child an early sense of the priority
    that the family places on faith and family as founda-
    tional to a person's integrated Catholic life.

❑ Children at the earliest ages should witness par-
    ents hugging, holding hands, and modeling other
    forms of healthy nonsexual touch.

Stage Three: Preschool 3–5 Years Old

Much of what we have already discussed is applicable
to children in this third stage of development. New actions and choices build upon what we have initiated in
our child's earliest two years. The infant/toddler generally
receives our teaching without too much resistance, but as
they grow through their "terrible two's" and into this age
group, a more "interactive" response from our children
about certain aspects of thinking, behavior, and expectations takes place.

As children enter this stage, they have begun to learn,
even if reluctantly, the rhythms, responsibilities, and relationships that are part of our Catholic family life.

Mentoring

❑ Establish structured "teaching times" where you
    read to your children from well-illustrated chil-
    dren's books — especially a children's Bible and
    books that introduce moral truth and virtue.

❑ Read good Christian books that teach lessons
    about sexuality in language and illustration that
    are age appropriate.

❑ There are many books — even for this age group — that promote non-Christian beliefs about family structure, sexual identity, and cultural norms about sexuality in general. Avoid them.

Modesty

❑ Begin teaching modesty in fashion, language, and behavior.

❑ Make certain your boundaries are consistent in application to both your sons and daughters.

❑ Beware of older siblings' inappropriate language, dress, or actions as influencers of younger children.

Privacy

❑ Teach the role of personal boundaries.

❑ A child's awareness of nudity is changing from the innocence of toddlerhood.

❑ Determine how you will deal with personal boundaries regarding individual versus group use of the toilet — that is, who is allowed to be in the bathroom when a child is using the toilet.

❑ Determine how you will handle showering, bathing, and dressing (alone, with parents, with siblings when very young, and so on).

❑ Determine how to apply personal boundaries when visiting relatives, friends, and public venues.

❑ Consider rules such as "always knock on closed doors before entering."

Touch

❑ Good touch is nonsexual touch (not intended to sexually arouse).

❑ Teach the child that some parts of body are "private parts," and no one should touch them (with obvious exception of parents and a physician with parents present).

- ❑ Secret touch is never okay (regardless of who is asking child to keep it secret).
- ❑ Keeping secrets about touch that is bad or is secret is not okay.
- ❑ No one should take pictures of the child's private parts.
- ❑ Begin teaching them to firmly say "no" to bad touch.
- ❑ Explain that bad touch can feel good but is still wrong.
- ❑ The rules never change regardless of the age of the perpetrator.

Technology

- ❑ Technology interests escalate during this age.
- ❑ No child should own or utilize digital technology without his or her parents' knowledge and participation.
- ❑ Accidental exposure to pornography can occur at this age. Be prepared with an explanation.
- ❑ All digital use is done together as a family, and not privately.
- ❑ Enforce no-screen times/days.
- ❑ Become aware of the technology that is available at others' homes, events, venues.
- ❑ Continue blocking software on all digital devices.

Modeling

- ❑ Consider curbing digital footprint in your home and lives (possibly cancel cable or movie channels).

❑ Provide nontech family entertainment or hobbies to relieve boredom and pent-up energy.

❑ Review your personal modesty, privacy, and media/entertainment habits.

Miscellaneous Tips

❑ Be prepared for awkward questions and situations.

❑ Have a planned response when asked about where babies come from (no storklike stories).

❑ Be ready to explain differences in parental and/or sibling genitalia.

Stage Four: School Ages 6–9 Years Old

This is the age where parents must begin being particularly strong in their parental commitment to mutually agreed upon standards, disciplined implementation of strategies, and transparency in their own lives as role models. Children will generally become more aware of and curious about sexually oriented topics. Their bodies are beginning to change, and you should become proactive in dealing with these issues as part of your continuous education and discussion about these topics. Also, the expanded universe of school, clubs, teams, and visiting other homes adds a much higher degree of susceptibility to pornography and inappropriate sexual information and experiences.

Mentoring

❑ Begin having broader discussions about life, its purpose, and paths to true happiness through holiness.

❑ Teach the benefits of purity, chastity, and sexual integrity.

- ❑ Share the meaning and importance of sacramental marriage and self-donating love.

- ❑ Do not accept the use of inappropriate language in general and sexual language in particular.

- ❑ Use more specific sexual terminology such as "making love" or "sexual intercourse." Using overly churchy terms like "marital embrace," or imprecise language like "having sex," doesn't work. Be clear.

- ❑ Use great books such as *Wonderfully Made Babies*, by Ellen Giangiordano and Dr. Lester Ruppersberger (for ages 9 and up).

- ❑ Include the spiritual and emotional — not just physical — context in talks concerning sex.

- ❑ Have clear discussions about the sexual maturing of their bodies and the corresponding physical effects.

- ❑ Discuss the temptations they will face in media, technology use, and social interactions and how to avoid the situations that facilitate sexual sin in these aspects of their lives.

- ❑ Set appropriate boundaries, and confirm the child's understanding of rules and boundaries and the consequences of ignoring them. Make sure this is a dialogue, not a monologue, to avoid any ambiguities or misunderstandings.

Technology

- ❑ Internet filtering should block any access to sexual content on every digital device in the home used by the child.

- ❑ Whole house solutions should be in place for routers, Wi-Fi, and similar technology.

❏ All passwords to every device should be known by parents and confirmed by parents regularly.

❏ Monitor all gaming and social websites.

Modeling

❏ Their bodies may be undergoing early adolescent changes, so be prepared to discuss and explain.

❏ Be prepared with a rational reason for boundaries and rules.

❏ Regularly review social media sites and history on your child's digital devices.

❏ Ensure you are staying free of pornography in every form.

❏ Enforce modesty standards regardless of gender of your children.

❏ Live sacramental and chaste adult lives.

❏ Participate in sacraments and involve your child.

❏ Involve your child in sacred traditions such as Holy Hour, works of mercy, volunteering.

Miscellaneous Tips

❏ The increased interaction with schools, teams, coaches, events, groups, classmates, and neighbors, as well as unprotected technology possessed by others, dramatically increases likelihood of encountering pornography. Be prepared for this exposure.

❏ Finally, as parents you should discuss together your child's nature. Extroverted or introverted? Socially popular or more of an outsider? Loner or joiner? Transparent or close to the vest? All of these aspects of your child's personality, temperament, and style help inform you regarding the various strategies you use on behalf of your children.

Stage Five: Adolescents 10–12 Years Old

As our children enter this period of their lives, they begin to transition from childhood to adolescence. Physical and emotional changes are moving quickly in this stage with the resulting awkwardness and intense introspection about their looks, peer respect, and self-image. The first significant stirrings of challenging rules, boundaries, and assumptions that you as parents have taught and enforced begin to be apparent. *Remember that this is the average age at which young people begin encountering pornography, so the threat becomes a significant issue.*

Spirituality becomes more important, but adolescents are heavily influenced by friends. Parents are particularly important as advocates for sexual integrity and as both models and mentors for their adolescents in helpful, direct ways. Many young people receive the sacrament of Confirmation during this stage. Let the experience be a real spiritual milestone in your child's life and a teaching opportunity to reinforce strong sexual morals.

Mentoring

This age group will generally receive your words and teaching with a certain degree of skepticism. The "do what I say" rationale is ineffective. Rather, parents must be prepared to discuss sexual issues and beliefs in an informed, logical, and compelling manner. All this can lead to some tension between parents and kids that without patience and a unified presentation between spouses can be challenging.

Instruction is often best done within the context of events and public personalities known to the child — for example, athletes, celebrities — who are in the news because of indiscretions or other sad circumstances. These represent real-life teaching moments that don't require the child to depend exclusively on the rationale of the parent, but rather demonstrate choices that have led to observably and objectively bad results.

When the sexual misconduct of cultural icons like rock stars, professional athletes, and others hits the media, the time is opportune to reference the event to reinforce earlier moral teachings. On the positive side, however, fantastic role models like retired professional baseball all-star Mike Sweeney, pro football San Diego Chargers quarterback Philip Rivers, and motion picture actor and producer Eduardo Verastegui are high-profile reminders of moral leadership in very public positions.

During this time, parents will need to:

- ❑ Have detailed discussions with their child about the basics of sexual intercourse.
- ❑ Discuss body image and the role it plays in impacting our decisions.
- ❑ Reinforce the consequences of actions taken.
- ❑ Teach the basics of human fertility and reproduction from a Catholic perspective.
- ❑ Reinforce the truth that the commitment found in marriage is the only appropriate environment for sexual activity.
- ❑ Differentiate between the cultural concept of love as a feeling and the truth of love as a choice and commitment.
- ❑ Begin to articulate the impact of porn in general and masturbation in particular on the brain from references such as can be found at www.fightthenewdrug.org.

❑ Introduce the concept of chastity and what it means as the norm for *all* persons.

❑ Discuss with simple illustrations the Church's teaching on homosexuality and other gender issues.

❑ Share various Catholic media presentations about sexuality and its proper role and beauty.

❑ Establish that group outings versus any sort of "dating" or relational exclusivity is the norm for this age.

Technology

Technology plays a huge role in the everyday life of this age group, and parents must take an active role in determining which, if any, personal technology their children may access, including and especially cell phones.

❑ Assess how tech savvy your child is in general to determine their level of tech sophistication.

❑ Determine rules and use of all digital devices and media.

❑ Take seriously the fact that this is the age where many children are confronted with porn for the first time.

❑ Consider the pros and cons of moving from blocking software to accountability software based on the maturity of your child. Software such Covenant Eyes (www.covenanteyes.com) will enable you to make that move appropriately on multiple devices.

❑ Enforce all tech boundaries such as no tech in closed rooms, surrendering of phones at night, and so on.

❏ Monitor all digital device usage including computers, games, social media, phones, music, and so forth.

❏ Require parental knowledge of all passwords and check them regularly but randomly.

Modeling

Consistency is at a high premium during these confusing and challenging days of your child's life. Parents must continue to show family solidarity and support. The spiritual life of the family is critical, incorporating continued sacramental living and active participation in the sacraments. Parents must share and live out spiritual lessons, and show how Jesus exercised compassion toward sinners while at the same time calling us to "sin no more."

❏ The importance of you, as parents, modeling a chaste lifestyle cannot be overstated.

❏ As a parent, you should begin to share your own real-life experiences that demonstrate how you chose to act in a moral manner in a difficult situation. Be as specific as possible. These real-life examples show your child that choosing specific moral actions applies to your life as well.

❏ Live sacramentally with full involvement in the parish and celebration of the sacraments with your kids.

Miscellaneous Tips

This is a time when both parents must watch for temperament changes and negative social experiences like bullying or social ostracizing. These social experiences are major life issues for children at this age and are also rampant in most of their social settings. At the first sign that your child is either the recipient or perpetrator of such actions, you must get involved. Children on the receiving end of such cruelty can begin to go silent and search for private "self-medication" through sexual acts such as masturbation that make them feel temporarily happy but end in secrecy and shame.

Stage Six: Teens Ages 13–18

This is the pinnacle of the attack on our children. This is the period of their lives where adherence to or violations of the principles you have imparted can have major consequences. It is a time for great prayer, hope, and encouragement on their behalf. Also, nearly all children have viewed pornography by the end of this age period.

Mentoring

- ❑ Have a full and detailed discussion of how pornography is targeted primarily at boys and the serious consequences to them of its use. Don't hold back.

- ❑ Have a full and detailed discussion of how pornography is growing in popularity with girls and how it objectifies and harms girls. In addition, girls need to be trained in how to avoid compromising situations with boys and the ramifications of premarital sex. Further, they need to learn how to hold young men responsible for treating them with dignity and respect.

- ❑ Teach abstinence and the purpose and benefits behind it. Again, I recommend reviewing the *Harmful Effects of Pornography 2016 Guide* found at Fight the New Drug website.

- ❑ Encourage accountability groups for teens through your local parish.

- ❏ Discuss the reality of terms like purity, chastity, and sexual integrity.
- ❏ The goal is to dialogue not preach, but this requires difficult listening.
- ❏ Discuss with your child his or her temperament, its strengths and weaknesses, and how to capitalize on the strengths and guard against the weaknesses.
- ❏ Discuss novelty, curiosity, societal eroticism, and peer pressure.
- ❏ Remind your children of your willingness to discuss anything at any time regarding sexuality.
- ❏ Review and reinforce your earlier detailed teaching on human sexuality and reproductive issues.
- ❏ Introduce the two purposes of marriage — procreative and unitive.
- ❏ Clearly differentiate between love and sex.
- ❏ Explain the benefits of boundaries surrounding dating or exclusive relationships.
- ❏ Help your children understand the benefits of healthy friendships and how to develop them with members of the opposite sex.
- ❏ Encourage them to help younger siblings by being an example.

Technology

- ❏ Move from blocking software to accountability software.
- ❏ Emphasize taking responsibility for one's choices and developing character.
- ❏ Continue following family technology rules and boundaries.

Modeling

❑ Ensure that all interactions between spouses are appropriate.

❑ Ensure that all interactions with friends of yours are appropriate and respectful.

❑ Diligently walk your talk. Kids at this age are watching every move you make.

❑ Investigate your child's friends, groups, clubs, teams, organizations, events, and hangouts.

❑ Praise and support your children at every opportunity, but especially when they choose wisely about curfews, behavior with the opposite sex, modesty, language, and so on. Be your child's biggest supporter.

❑ Be a parent. Being a "buddy" will come later.

Miscellaneous Tip

If younger siblings are in the home, differentiate rules based on age. This can cause some internal strife if children are in different life stages. Be prepared to explain.

A Final Comment about Scripts

Virtually every time I speak about pornography, parents come up after the talk, and by far their first question is this: "What, exactly, do I say when I explain sex to my kids?" The second most common question is: "How do I talk to my kids about pornography?" These are two great questions and could take an entire book in themselves to answer.

Essentially, these parents are asking me for scripts. But there are a lot of variables to consider regarding the first question — how to speak about sex — including whether you are a person of faith who wants to reinforce Christian beliefs about sexuality, or to speak in a more secular, nuts-and-bolts, biological manner; the age of your child; whether you have talked about sexuality at all in their earlier years; and so on. At the very least, when these questions come up in a post-talk setting, I suggest that parents consult their pediatrician and priest to get a balanced approach.

My wife and I felt that in our experience clear, concise, biological information needed to be connected to biblical and spiritual teachings. As Catholics, we included the teachings and recommendations of the Catholic faith. We consulted books, professionals, and clergy for their input.

Pornography is a much different topic. As I have been insisting throughout this book, at various stages of a child's life you must proactively protect them with technology, practices, mentoring, and modeling, as we have discussed. However, at each stage (usually around age seven or eight), you must begin discussions about the dangers of porn *and* the benefits of purity and sexual integrity. I know it feels as if this a very young age for this teaching — and that's your call — but do not bury your head in the sand and think they are not being targeted by pornographers. They are. Use the conversations and push-back from your kids about boundaries and rules as prime opportunities for age-appropriate explanations regarding *why* you are putting these guidelines into effect.

As we discussed earlier, science has given us tremendous insight into the effects of pornography on the brain. You can begin to explain, in simple language, the basic information about how the brain responds to stimuli with kids who are in the seven- to nine-year-old range. As children get a bit older, I have found that discussions about how the brain works relative to the dangers of pornography, and how it is radically and negatively affected and wounded by pornography, is a compelling way to explain the problems of pornography as well as the benefits of remaining chaste.

The bottom line is that our conversations with our children were unique to our beliefs and choices. What is universally true, however, is that: 1) you must have these conversations; 2) the discussions must be age-appropriate and clear; and 3) such discussions should be handled by both mothers and fathers who affirm the dignity, sacredness, and beauty with which God created our bodies and the ultimate end for which we were created. I would highly recommend reading material from or contacting various clergy, lay apostolates, and Catholic professionals who can give you great advice on these discussions.

The number one influence on children throughout their lives is you, the parent. You have a critical role to play — don't sit it out.

Conclusion

We have highlighted some major steps you can employ to successfully help your children attain a healthy and holy sexual outlook and experience in their lives. It is critical to remember that the number one influence on children throughout their lives is you, the parent. You have a critical role to play — don't sit it out.

I close with a quote from the Archbishop of Kansas City in Kansas, Archbishop Joseph F. Naumann, who in the archdiocesan anti-pornography initiative workbook for his priests, religious, and Catholic families wrote this:

> In every age the Gospel stands for human life and dignity. Today, when one of the greatest assaults

on our dignity comes from the degradation of human sexuality, Catholics and others of good will can transform society through lives of joyful chastity. With faith in the Father who created us, the Son who redeemed us, and the Holy Spirit who sustains us, let us now accept that challenge.

The information found in this section is the result of personal experience and research on scores of different health, Christian, and government websites, including but not limited to: HealthyChildren.org of the American Academy of Pediatrics, © 2013; The National Sexual Resource Center, Inc., © 2013; the *Parenting the Internet Generation* e-book from Covenant Eyes, Inc., © 2016; various diocesan websites; and from an adaption of *Human Sexuality — A Catholic Perspective for Education and Lifelong Learning*, © 1991, United States Catholic Conference of Bishops.

Luke Gilkerson of Covenant Eyes, Inc., has created a wonderful book called *The Talk: 7 Lessons to Introduce Your Child to Biblical Sexuality*. I received further assistance from psychologist Dr. Todd Bowman and his book *Angry Birds and Killer Bees: Talking to Your Kids about Sex*. Additional resources of particular benefit include *Good Pictures Bad Pictures* by Kristen Jenson and Gail Poyner, *Wonderfully Made! Babies* by Ellen Giangiordano and Dr. Lester Ruppersberger, and the information found on www.FightThe-NewDrug.org.

Afterword

So there you have it, a few stories, thoughts, and strategies for dealing with a very significant and worrisome problem we all face as parents. I hope my ideas will be of some value to you as you confront the challenge that pornography poses to your family and especially to your children.

We live in trying times, and nothing more clearly reveals the problems and deep sadness of our age than does pornography, which has embedded itself in our culture in such a way that it has become pervasive and yet — paradoxically — hardly noticed. You, however, have noticed, or you would not be holding this book in your hands. The fact that you have noticed gives me great hope.

Our children are our future, but they must be loved, protected, and fiercely defended until they are capable of embodying that future. As a father, I have been deeply aware of that fact for years, and it was that awareness that spurred me to write this book. Our young people deserve all that the world can give them, but the world at this particular moment seems unable to distinguish between giving our children a piece of bread or a stone, a fish or a snake — it's all the same, apparently. So it becomes our job as parents to do the work that the world declines to do.

I want to encourage you in your efforts and will offer many, many prayers on your behalf, and especially on behalf of the children you love and defend. I urge you to fight on and to not lose hope. The going may be rough at times, but if you are patient, you will eventually persevere and your children will be able to grow up unscathed and undamaged. They will become the persons they were meant to be, and that will bring you great joy.

You will persevere, by the way, because you fight on the right side of things — the side of love. Love is at the heart of all reality, which means that despite what it might look like, despite what the world might tell you, you will win, and your children will go on to become the healthy and happy individuals you pray for them to become.

The appendixes that follow provide various tools to help you in this battle. To get started in building your integrated Catholic family culture, use the "assessment" provided in appendix B. May God bless you, your marriage, and your children.

Appendixes

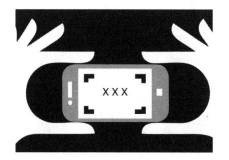

Resources to Help You Fight the Fight

Please note: *The resources listed here are not to be considered an endorsement of any service or product. Users should investigate and choose the best option for their family as they deem necessary.*

CATHOLIC CHURCH DOCUMENTS

Create in Me A Clean Heart, United States Conference of Catholic Bishops, www.usccb.org

As for Me and My House, Archbishop Joseph F. Naumann, Kansas City, Kansas, www. archkck.org/myhouse

Bought with a Price, Bishop Paul Loverde, Arlington, Virginia, www. asldkjfa.org

Into the Breach, Bishop Thomas J. Olmstead, Phoenix, Arizona, www.dphx.org

WEBSITES

My House anti-pornography program: www.archkck.org/myhouse

National Center on Sexual Exploitation: www.endsexualexploitation.org

Integrity Restored: www.integrityrestored.com

Reclaim Sexual Health: www.reclaimsexualhealth.com

Enough is Enough: www.enough.org

Faithful & True: www.faithfulandtrue.com

Matt Fradd: www.theporneffect.com

Overcoming Pornography: www.overcomingpornography.org

Pure Hope: www.purehope.net

I Keep Safe: www.ikeepsafe.org

Focus on the Family: www.focusonthefamily.com

Dirty Girls Ministries: www.dirtygirls.com

United States Conference of Catholic Bishops: www.usccb.org

Plugged In Online: www.pluggedinonline.com

Chastity Project: www.chastityproject.com

Family Honor: www.familyhonor.org

Leah Darrow: www.leahdarrow.com

Dr. Laura Heap MD: www.ruhealthyruhappy.com

Fight the New Drug: www.fightthenewdrug.org/

Women for Decency: www.womenfordecency.org

Internet Safety 101: www.internetsafety101.org/

Facebook for Parents: facebookforparents.org/

Internet Safety Resources: www.txssc.txstate.edu/K12/internet-safety

Beauty Redefined: www.beautyredefined.net/

Focus on the Family: www.focusonthefamily.com/parenting/sexuality.aspx

Decent Films: www.decentfilms.com

Porn Proof Kids: www.pornproofkids.com

Good Pictures Bad Pictures: www.goodpicturesbadpictures.com

MARRIAGE SUPPORT

Marriage Encounter: www.wwme.com

For Your Marriage: www.foryourmarriage.org

The Alexander House: www.thealexanderhouse.org (for healing marriages)

Retrouvaille: www.retrouvaille.org (for troubled marriages)

TECHNOLOGY

Covenant Eyes: www.covenanteyes.com

Reclaim Sexual Health: www.reclaimsexualhealth.com (online program)

BSafe: www.bsafe.com

Safe Eyes: www.safeeyes.com

Phone Sheriff: www.phonesheriff.com

My Mobile Watchdog: www.mymobilewatchdog.com

Ad Block: www.adblock.com/en/chrome

41 Pounds: www.41Pounds.org (catalog cancelling service)

Kyte Phone: www.Kytephone.com

Open DNS Family Shield: www.opendns.com (wireless home blocking system)

iPhantom: www.iphantom.com (malware blocking system)

Pandora's Hope: www.pandorashope.com (home router with monitoring)

K9 Web Protection: www.k9webprotection.com (protection on devices)

Accountable 2 You: www.accountable2you.com (whole house, all device protection)

MobiCip: www.mobicip.com (device protection)

BOOKS

Good Pictures Bad Pictures. Kristen Jenson and Gail Poyner. Glen Cove Press, 2014.

Wonderfully Made! Babies. Ellen Giangiordano and Dr. Lester Ruppersberger. Create Space Independent Publishing Platform, 2014.

Love & Responsibility. Karol Wojtyla (Pope St. John Paul II). Ignatius Press.

Good News about Sex & Marriage. Christopher West.

Be a Man. Father Larry Richards.

The Catholic Family Handbook. Rev. George A. Kelly. New York: Random House, Inc., 1959.

Dr. Ray Guarendi Parenting books
  * *Winning the Disciplining Debates*
  * *When Faith Causes Family Friction*
  * *Good Discipline, Great Teens*

Dr. James C. Dobson parenting books
  * *The New Dare to Discipline*

- *Bringing Up Boys*
- *Preparing for Adolescence: How to Survive the Coming Years of Change*
- *Building Confidence in Your Child*

Dr. Gregory K. Popcak and Lisa Popcak marriage and parenting books

- *Parenting with Grace: A Guide to Raising Almost Perfect Kids*
- *Just Married: The Catholic Guide to Surviving and Thriving in the First Five Years of Marriage*
- *Then Baby Comes: The Catholic Guide to Surviving and Thriving in the First Three Years of Parenthood*

Meg Meeker, M.D., parenting books

- *Strong Mothers, Strong Sons: Lessons Mothers Need to Raise Extraordinary Men*
- *Strong Fathers, Strong Daughters: 10 Secrets Every Father Should Know*
- *Your Kids at Risk: How Teen Sex Threatens Our Sons and Daughters*

In the Shadow of the Net. Patrick Carnes.

Every Man's Battle: Winning the War on Sexual Temptation One Victory at a Time, Stephen Arterburn and Fred Stoeker

Every Young Man's Battle. Stephen Arterburn and Fred Stoeker.

Preparing Your Son for Everyman's Battle, Stephen Arterburn and Fred Stoeker

Integrity Restored, Helping Catholics Win the Battle against Pornography. Peter Kleponis, Ph.D. Emmaus Road, 2014.

Real Love. Mary Beth Bonacci. Ignatius Press.

If You Really Loved Me. Jason Evert. St. Anthony Messenger Press. https://shop.franciscanmedia.org

The Pornography Epidemic, A Catholic Approach. Peter Kleponis, Ph.D. Simon Peter Press, Inc., 2012,

Pure Desire. Ted Roberts, Regal Books, Inc. 1999.

Breaking Free, 12 Steps to Sexual Purity for Men. Stephen Wood. Family Life Center Publications. www.familylifecenter.net

Protecting Your Child in an X-Rated World, What You Need to Know to Make a Difference. Frank York and Jan LaRue. Tyndale House Publishers. www.family.org

The Temperament God Gave Your Kids: Motivate, Love and Discipline Your Kids. Art and Larraine Bennett, Our Sunday Visitor Publishing, 2012.

Delivered: True Stories of Men and Women Who Turned from Porn to Purity. Edited by Matt Fradd.

Healing the Wounds of Sexual Addiction. Dr. Mark Laaser. Harper Collins.

Wild at Heart Field Manual. John Eldredge. Thomas Nelson, 2001.

The Way of the Wild Heart (book and workbook). John Eldredge. Thomas Nelson, 2006.

Healing the Hardware of the Soul. Dr. Daniel Amen. SPECT Scans.

Don't Call It Love: Recovery from Sexual Addiction. Patrick Carnes.

Out of the Shadows. Patrick Carnes.

The Wounded Heart. Dan Allender.

E-BOOKS

Parenting the Internet Generation. Covenant Eyes, Inc. www.CovenantEyes.com/ebooks/

Pornography Use and Recovery, Covenant Eyes, Inc. www.CovenantEyes.com/ebooks/

Your Brain on Porn. Covenant Eyes, Inc., www.CovenantEyes.com/e-books

VIDEOS AND DVDs

Renewing the Mind of the Media. United States Conference of Catholic Bishops. www.usccb.org

Winning the Battle for Sexual Purity. Christopher West. www.LuminousMedia.org

Sex & Young America, The Real Deal. Coalition for the Protection of Children and Families.

Real Love — The Video Series. Mary Beth Bonacci.

Every Young Man's Battle. Family Life Center Publications. www .familylifecenter.net

Archdiocese of Kansas City in Kansas anti-pornography video. www.archkck.org/myhouse (free to view online)

THERAPISTS

Dr. Peter Kleponis: www.integrityrestored.com

Dr. Mark Laaser: www.faithfulandtrue.com

Dr. Todd Bowman: www.satpinstitute.com

HELP GROUPS

Sexaholics Anonymous: www.sa.org

Sex Addicts Anonymous: www.saa.org

Sex and Love Addicts Anonymous: www.slaafws.org

MEN'S GROUPS

St. Joseph Covenant Keepers: www.dads.com

That Man Is You: www.paradisusdei.org

Fathers of St. Joseph: www.fathersofstjoseph.org

WOMEN'S GROUPS

Dirty Girls Ministries: www.dirtygirlsministries.com

Women of Grace: www.womenofgrace.com

GENERAL ACCOUNTABILITY GROUP QUESTIONS

Accountability Group Questions: Accountability@StJosephCenter. com

CDs

The Pornography Plague. Jeff Cavins. www.LuminousMedia.org

God, Sex and the Meaning of Life. Christopher West. Ascension Press.

Checklist for a Spiritually Healthy Family

	Never	**Sometimes**	**Always**

Does your family pray together?

	1	2	3

Does your family celebrate Mass together and participate in the life of the parish?

	1	2	3

Does your family enjoy regular meals together?

	1	2	3

Do the parents set rules and expectations for the children regarding such things as telephone and computer use, video games, study time, and curfews?

	1	2	3

Do the parents monitor and limit what the children are allowed to watch on television?

	1	2	3

Are all computers and televisions within the home in open and visible places and not in children's bedrooms?

	1	2	3

Does your family regularly participate together in activities aimed at physical and mental development?

	1	2	3

Do the parents make wise and virtuous centered choices about their own entertainment, including television, movies, reading material, and the Internet?

	1	2	3

Do the parents both publicly and privately model the kind of behavior they want their children to emulate?

1	2	3

Will parents seek or recommend pastoral or professional care if needed and will be advocates?

1	2	3

Total   ____   ____   ____

Score of 25–30: Very concerned about making good choices for yourself and your family.

Score of 15–24: Your family might benefit from better monitoring.

Score less than 15: You should consider making some positive changes for yourself and your family.

Source: Archdiocese of Kansas City in Kansas, *As for Me and My House*, Leadership Manual, pp. 73–74

APPENDIX C

Prayers for Divine Protection and Assistance

ST. MICHAEL THE ARCHANGEL

St. Michael the Archangel, defend us in battle.

Be our defense against the wickedness and snares of the Devil.

May God rebuke him, we humbly pray, and do thou, O Prince of the heavenly hosts,

by the power of God, thrust into hell Satan, and all the evil spirits, who prowl about the world

seeking the ruin of souls. Amen.

CONFITEOR

I confess to almighty God

and to you, my brothers and sisters,

that I have greatly sinned,

in my thoughts and in my words,

in what I have done and in what I have failed to do,

through my fault, through my fault,

through my most grievous fault;

therefore I ask blessed Mary ever-Virgin,

all the Angels and Saints,

and you, my brothers and sisters,

to pray for me to the Lord our God.

MORNING OFFERING

O Jesus, through the immaculate heart of Mary, I offer you all my prayers, works, joys, and sufferings of this day in union with the holy sacrifice of the Mass throughout the world. I offer them for all the intentions of your Sacred Heart: the salvation of souls, reparation for sin, the reunion of all Christians. I offer them for the intentions of our bishops and of all the apostles of prayer, and in particular for those recommended by our Holy Father this month. Amen.

A Prayer against Pornography

Lord, technology has helped the world in many ways, but it has also proven to be a snare into sin through the lure of pornography. We ask a hedge of protection against this temptation that has the power to damage families and scar the spirit of both the one who views pornography and those who love those caught up in this trap.

Help keep our minds on You in such a powerful way that pornography holds no allure. Give us the wisdom to remove temptations that we cannot resist, and to always keep You first in our hearts and minds. Amen.

A Prayer for Rebellious Youth

Dear Lord, you have witnessed the rebelliousness of youth since the very beginnings of time. You understand a parent's anguish and helplessness over the actions of his child.

Please help us to transform our anger and frustration into loving care for our child who has gone astray. Help us begin to mend our broken fences and heal our broken hearts. Bless our child and also help him to mend the error of his ways. Help and bless us all to do right in Your name and restore us to peace and tranquility. Amen.

Sample Online Accountability Checklist

Have you discussed and set up online guidelines for your family?

Y   **N**

Do your kids have social media accounts?

Y   **N**

If yes, which ones (circle):

Facebook

Twitter

Instagram

Snapchat

Myspace

YouTube

Ning

Tagged

Pinterest

MeetMe (formerly myYearbook)

Foursquare

Google+

LinkedIn

Flickr

Blogger

WordPress

Other

For each social media account that they have, do I have an account and "friend" or "follow" my kids online?

Y   **N**

You need to be aware what photos, information, and interactions your kids are having online. This is where most of their online interaction happens.

SOCIAL MEDIA

Are the social media account privacy settings set appropriately?

$$\textbf{Y} \qquad \textbf{N}$$

For each account can you restrict how the content is viewed by the Internet and a complete stranger?

$$\textbf{Y} \qquad \textbf{N}$$

Have you discussed "Think before you post" with your kids?

$$\textbf{Y} \qquad \textbf{N}$$

Think before you post, text, tweet, tag, or e-mail any information. Once you press "send," you can't get it back.

SOCIAL NETWORKING

Do your kids use instant messaging? (Facebook Messenger, Skype, iChat, MSN Messenger)

$$\textbf{Y} \qquad \textbf{N}$$

If yes, have you reviewed their list of friends or contacts?

$$\textbf{Y} \qquad \textbf{N}$$

Do your kids use chat rooms?

$$\textbf{Y} \qquad \textbf{N}$$

INTERNET SAFETY

Do you and your family know how to recognize phishing schemes?

$$\textbf{Y} \qquad \textbf{N}$$

Beware of pop-ups, e-mails from service providers, banks, and sweep-stakes — any ploy for an attacker to seem trusted when all they really want is your information.

Do you and your family know how to browse the Internet safely?

$$\textbf{Y} \qquad \textbf{N}$$

SAFE WEB SURFING

Don't be click happy; beware of pirating software; beware of "free" software.

Do you and your family know what personal information is?

$$\text{Y} \qquad \text{N}$$

Birthday (with year), address, phone number, mother's maiden name, social security number, usernames, and passwords

Do you and/or your family shop online?

$$\text{Y} \qquad \text{N}$$

Where do you enter your credit card? My rule: Fortune 500, hospital, financial institution, otherwise use a gift card.

Do you and/or your family bank online?

$$\text{Y} \qquad \text{N}$$

Do you have a strong password? Is it different than other online accounts?

$$\text{Y} \qquad \text{N}$$

Do you know how to create a strong password?

$$\text{Y} \qquad \text{N}$$

When was the last time you changed your passwords?

If it has been more than six months, change them now.

Adapted from Secure,
Cathy Olsen, ©Securemama.com

Sample Parental Purity Pledge

I _____ commit that I will not be part of the pornographic plague in any way, nor allow my spouse or children to become a victim to the full extent of my ability.

I will do this by:

- Educating myself on the harms of pornography to self, spouse, and family.

- Learning to recognize the red flags of pornography so as to avoid such traps.

- Engaging in open, honest discussions about pornography with those in my family.

- Seeking help from priests and trained counselors if ever our family needs help.

- Promising to refrain from all inappropriate sexual practices within my marriage.

- Promising to not engage in any interaction with pornography at all.

- Promising to pray for my spouse and my children regularly.

- Clearly define what all guidelines and boundaries are for our family.

- Avoid inappropriate actions or comments toward persons of the opposite sex.

- Never make light of or joke about sexuality, pornography, or purity.

_____ (Signature)

_____ (Date)

Acknowledgments

It is almost as daunting a task to thank those who were so instrumental in this book coming to fruition as it was to pen the entire book. That being said, and in the fear of forgetting someone, I would be remiss not to acknowledge those who thought more of my ability to do this than I ever did.

- When Mike Aquilina and I were both speaking at a men's conference a number of years ago, he made what seemed like an impossible suggestion: to write a book on the topic of pornography. A topic so challenging that just speaking of it made both me and my audiences feel uneasy at best. But when Mike, the author or editor of more than forty books, made his suggestion, I initially took it as a joke — like a world-class artist encouraging a blind man to paint. Easy for you to say, I thought. But he was serious. Mike became the catalyst that initiated my journey into writing this book. He was, and remains, a man of great encouragement. I am extraordinarily thankful for being the recipient of such friendship and support.

- None of this would ever have been possible without the uncompromisingly bullish attitude of my lovely wife, Linda. Her down-to-earth spirituality was expressed simply and frequently in her no-nonsense insistence to "just do it." Her absolute belief spurred me on during many a worrisome night of writing. It was the same with our four grown children — Erin, Dan, David, and Kelly — as well as their faith-filled spouses. All seemed to conspire in repeating the "You can do it" mantra. Likewise, my parents, Dan and Jane Spencer, who never doubted the outcome of this project even while struggling to believe our society had come to need such a book.

- Friends like Kevin Lowry, Rod Handley, Mike Sweeney, and Tony Collins gave both encouragement and guidance to my task. They are friends who, in the spirit of Christian brotherhood, continually shared the importance of the message, instructive insights to its crafting, and rock solid belief in its much needed voice in a troubled world.

- Professionals in the field of healing individuals and families from the nightmare of pornography like Dr. Peter Kleponis and Dr. Todd Bowman (both authors of books of great value in this field) were indispensable in their commitment to the message of hope. Sam Meier, lead counselor and consultant in one of the nation's first and leading diocesan pro-marriage and anti-pornography initiatives — My House, in the Archdiocese of Kansas City in Kansas — was unconditionally supportive and patient in reviewing my manuscript and offering constructive suggestions.

- In my many national travels to speak on the challenges of pornography, I was particularly blessed by friends such as Peter Quirk and Lou Piazza, both of the Archdiocese of New Orleans, along with two extraordinary clerics: Fr. Joseph Palermo and the Most Reverend Gregory M. Aymond, Archbishop of New Orleans, who provided multiple opportunities for me to address the issue in their archdiocese.

- No literary effort is successful without the skills of essential supporting cast such as my agent Gail Coniglio, former Our Sunday Visitor acquisition editor Cindy Cavnar, the whole Our Sunday Visitor team, and editor John Collins, who all helped me shape a mass of unorganized chaos into a coherent whole.

- Last but not least, my prayerful thanks to Pope St. John Paul II and the Catholic Church, whose teachings on the dignity, purpose, and beauty of human sexuality are so essential to understanding this truth in an increasingly confused and wounded world. Also to the heroic, visionary, and humble Archbishop Joseph F. Naumann, whose tireless championing of authentic love, marriage, and the family through his leadership of the Church in my Archdiocese of Kansas City, Kansas, has been and continues to be an enormous personal witness and inspiration to me.

- No acknowledgments would be truly complete without a nod to Riley, my beloved canine companion, who kept me calm in the stressful times of writing with undeserved devotion.

Notes

1. Great leadership has been shown by shepherds like Archbishop Joseph F. Naumann of Kansas City, Kansas; Bishop Paul Loverde of Arlington, Virginia; Archbishop Daniel Amen of New Orleans, Louisiana; Bishop Thomas Olmsted of Phoenix, Arizona; and many others.

2. 2010 Family Safe Media report.

3. Covenant Eyes, *Protecting Your Family Online* booklet, 2013.

4. Ibid.

5. My House anti-pornography initiative, 2005, Archdiocese of Kansas City in Kansas, parish video.

6. Cheryl B. Aspy et al., "Parental Communication and Youth Sexual Behavior," *Journal of Adolescence* 30 (2007): 449–466.

7. Vincent Guilamo-Ramos et al., "Parental Expertise, Trustworthiness, and Accessibility: Parent-Adolescent Communication and Adolescent Risk Behavior," *Journal of Marriage and Family* 68, no. 5 (December 2006): 1229–1246.

8. *Catechism of the Catholic Church* 2223.

9. National Center for Health Statistics Report, July 2015.

10. Cheryl B. Aspy et al., "Parental Communication and Youth Sexual Behavior," *Journal of Adolescence* 30 (2007): 449–466.

11. Vincent Guilamo-Ramos et al., "Parental Expertise, Trustworthiness, and Accessibility: Parent-Adolescent Communication and Adolescent Risk Behavior," *Journal of Marriage and Family* 68, no. 5 (December 2006): 1229–1246.